Echoes of Hope

How the Message of the Prophets Still Lingers Today

Contents

Introduction

As someone who has studied language and how to teach it, I've seen how words and their context matter greatly. A statement like "I have the keys" may not sound important but could evoke strong emotions in someone who has been searching frantically for them. Relief—the search is over. Frustration—all this time searching! Anger—why didn't you tell me you had them?!

Our expectations for words vary, too. While my one-year-old daughter can get by with just saying "milk" when she's thirsty, I expect my three-year old to make her request at least a little more polite. Technical terms may quickly lose their audience in casual conversation but could fit perfectly in a conversation in a lab. A job application riddled with grammatical errors might cost the applicant a work opportunity even if the person were otherwise qualified for the job.

In much the same way, knowing the context for what we read in the Bible makes a huge difference for understanding it. The literary style varies, and the culture of the time impacts it as well. It's easy to focus on passages we like while skipping over parts that aren't in narrative form or seem more removed from our lives today.

Let's be honest—there are many passages in the prophets that seem difficult because they talk about hard things. The people of Israel and Judah continued to turn away from God despite the repeated warnings of the prophets. Both nations were punished for their sin and many of the prophets faced significant challenges. And yet, in spite of the warnings and judgment, we still see an incredible message of hope for future restoration throughout these books.

We may struggle to see ourselves in these texts, especially of being guilty of the same core sins that tripped up the people of Judah and Israel. We gloss over their idolatry as being antiquated and far removed from our society. We don't like to acknowledge that while the idols of our culture may be less tangible than the ones worshiped in the time of the prophets, they can pull our hearts away from the Lord just as much. The passages on justice can make us equally uncomfortable due to tensions between what different groups view as justice today.

In this study, we'll look at an overview of the prophetic books traditionally found in Isaiah through Malachi in our English Bibles. These books have a lot of content, and I hope you'll see major themes that span them and gain a better understanding of the writing styles used. We'll also look at the major message repeated throughout these books and how it still matters for us all these years later.

When you get to passages that say **read** in bold, I hope you take the time to look these up and read them in your Bible. I want you to get to spend time studying them for yourself instead of just reading about them in this book. For the sake of time, though, you'll see other passages marked with "See…" If you have time to read those they'll give you more context, but aren't required for completing this Bible study.

I hope as you read and study, God will illuminate passages He wants to use to speak to you today. As with the keys example earlier, different readings may draw out different emotions in each of us based on our personal experiences. And at the same time, I hope you'll see how each of the prophets point us in the same direction—toward the hope we have in Jesus.

Rebecca

About the Author

Rebecca Rechner loves studying God's word and seeing the connections throughout the Bible making it one unified story. While she has always loved writing, God prompted her to start writing a Bible study in late 2019 right after her youngest daughter was born. After several years of research, writing, and editing, usually late at night or on weekends, you're holding the final product in your hands. You can also find her blog at in-perfect-peace.com where she shares about her life and what God's teaching her. She lives in central Illinois with her husband and three daughters.

The Prophetic Era

Session 1
The Backdrop

THE ROLE OF THE PROPHETS

"Now listen! Today I am giving you a choice between life and death, between prosperity and disaster. For I command you this day to love the LORD your God and to keep his commands, decrees, and regulations by walking in His ways. If you do this, you will live and multiply, and the LORD your God will bless you and the land you are about to enter and occupy. But if your heart turns away and you refuse to listen, and if you are drawn away to serve and worship other gods, then I warn you now that you will certainly be destroyed. You will not live a long, good life in the land you are crossing the Jordan to occupy."
– Deuteronomy 30:15-18

I love a good story. Good guys, bad guys, plot twists, problems to solve. And in the end, good had better win, every time. On the rare occasion I read a book with a sad or unresolved ending, I tend to feel disgruntled and a bit cheated. Sure, real life is messy and rarely has those happy endings, but that's what a book is for, right? Escape from reality for a bit where good can triumph even when it's just fiction. And even more so when it's a biography of a real person. I cheer on the good side all the way to the end and can feel just as fiercely loyal to the people as if they were truly my friends.

Even if you aren't an avid reader, chances are you're familiar with at least some of the narrative stories that make up about 43 percent of the Bible.[i] They're much easier to read than the poetry and prose discourse literary styles that make up the remaining 33 percent and 24 percent of the Bible respectively.[ii] In these stories we can read about people like Noah, Moses, Joshua, Ruth, David, and so many more. And if we focus on the Sunday School versions, they usually have a hero or heroine we want to come out on top.

In reality, if we look closer, the true hero type is harder to find in the pages of the Bible as it captures the failings and not-quite-there moments for these people. And over and over, the Bible tells us there will be One who *is* that hero. Several times it seems we may have stumbled across that person in the Old Testament, but each time, we're left still waiting and wanting. Many of these promises of this future hero come from the prophets that we'll focus on in this study.

Before we go any further, what comes to your mind when you think of the word "**prophet**"? Why?

Thinking about prophets, what names come to mind, if any?

Merriam-Webster defines a prophet as "one who utters divinely inspired revelations," "one gifted with more than ordinary spiritual and moral insight," or "one who foretells future events."[iii] Throughout the Old Testament, we see references to prophets, men of God, and seers who told people what God wanted them to do, or what was coming. Many were men, such as Samuel and Elijah, but some were also women including Deborah and Huldah. In many of the earlier stories, we see how God used the prophets to tell the people how He planned to save them from trouble and then how He fulfilled those promises.

As we get further into the Old Testament story, we see a shift in the prophets' messages. During that time, several foreign empires rose and fell but through each of them, God spoke the same general message through the prophets to His people:

Warning. You have broken your part of the LORD's covenant. Repent!

Judgment when they didn't repent.

And yet, **Hope** that even in spite of their rebellion, God still loved them and wanted to restore not only Judah and Israel, but *all* nations.[iv]

Just as many of the earlier prophets spoke of God's coming salvation, the later prophets still point to that. Unfortunately, they had to include a caveat that the people's behavior could interfere with God's ongoing desire to save His people. If they heeded the prophets' warnings and turned back to God, He would still offer hope and salvation. But if they chose not to repent, then they would experience consequences for their disobedience. Even in their punishment, though, God still had a plan to bless His people in the future. All was not lost.

So, God sent prophets to point His people back to following His way. We don't know how He led all of them into this role, but we're going to read God's call to Ezekiel as an example of what He asked them to do. As you read, try to put yourself in Ezekiel's shoes.

Read Ezekiel 2:1-3:14. Jot down anything that stands out to you as you read.

We'll spend more time on Ezekiel when we get to the time of the Babylonian empire, but as a quick summary, he had been exiled to Babylon along with many others from Judah, probably around 597 BC.[v] In the midst of what would have already been an unsettling time for Ezekiel, God called him to a task that sounds overwhelming to me. With the reminder that the Israelites had been rebelling against God for generations, God sent Ezekiel to tell the people to return to the LORD.

Did you notice how many times God reminded Ezekiel to obey Him whether the people listened or not? And in 3:4-8, God made it clear the people *wouldn't* listen. But He assured Ezekiel He had prepared him for this and told him not to be afraid of how the people responded.

Maybe in some ways knowing this could be a relief to Ezekiel when it seemed like his words fell on deaf ears. And yet, how draining and discouraging it must have been. As a priest from the tribe of Levi (see Ezekiel 1:2-3), Ezekiel would most likely have known God's law, seen firsthand how the people ignored it, and witnessed the tragic result.

Did you also notice how God emphasized that He had called Ezekiel to his own people who spoke his own language? They were living in a foreign land where the people spoke a different language, but God had not called Ezekiel to reach the Babylonians. Even in the midst of their punishment, God was still pursuing His people, trying to get them to turn back to Him.

As we read, you'll also see mentions of false prophets who generally told the people and kings what they wanted to hear. While prophets like Ezekiel warned of God's punishment for sin, false prophets reassured the people they could keep doing what they wanted. In Deuteronomy 18, in one of the passages where we also see a promise of a prophet to come later, God gave the people a litmus test for knowing if a prophet is true.

> **Read Deuteronomy 18:15-22.** How were the people to know whether a prophet was truly sent by God?

God's true prophets didn't necessarily live long enough to see how God did everything He told them He would do. Yet, as the story of Israel and Judah unfolds in the Bible, we can see how God vindicated His prophets' words as He did exactly what He promised through them.

We still have to be on the lookout for false prophets today. Just because someone says they have a word from God doesn't mean they really do, no matter how influential they may be or what position they may have in a church. While time will tell whether their words come true, we can also test their message against the pages of scripture. If their words go against God's written word, we can be sure the LORD did not send them.

One popular false message in today's culture is sometimes called the prosperity gospel. This false narrative says if we do everything right, God will give us health, wealth and success in all we do. In this study, we'll see over and over how God promised to bless His people for obeying Him, but that didn't mean, and still doesn't today, that He would prevent all bad things from happening to them. We still live in a fallen world this side of heaven.

We live in challenging times, but our God is the same yesterday, today, and forever. The LORD's message to us today is the same one we'll see spoken through the prophets. God calls us to pursue righteousness and warns of the consequences if we don't.

Following God may require denying ourselves what we think we want, but there is hope on the other side. It reminds me of these words from Isaiah 55:6-8, which say:

> *"Seek the LORD while you can find Him.*
> *Call on Him now while He is near.*
> *Let the wicked change their ways*
> *and banish the very thought of doing wrong.*
> *Let them turn to the LORD that He may have mercy on them.*
> *Yes, turn to our God, for He will forgive generously.*
> *'My thoughts are nothing like your thoughts,' says the LORD.*
> *'And my ways are far beyond anything you could imagine.'"*

Walking with the LORD is a journey, but the first step always comes back to seeking God. And seeking Him means following the path He leads us down, trusting He'll be faithful to us just as He was to Ezekiel. Faithful even when the path doesn't look anything like we expected. I'm confident we'll each find that to be true.

> Is there anything God has asked you to do that you've tried to ignore or explain away? If yes, in what area(s)?

Ask the LORD to open your eyes to what He has to show you through this study. Jot down anything that comes to mind as you pray. Depending on what you wrote to answer the last question, you may also want to spend some time taking that before God in prayer.

Day 2

THE COVENANT

"Understand, therefore, that the LORD your God is indeed God. He is the faithful God who keeps his covenant for a thousand generations and lavishes his unfailing love on those who love him and obey his commands. But he does not hesitate to punish and destroy those who reject him. Therefore, you must obey all these commands, decrees, and regulations I am giving you today."
– Deuteronomy 7:9-11

When I was young, my parents bought a beautiful set of encyclopedias and if I wanted to learn about something, I had to find the right book and know how to spell the word to see if it was included. Once I found it, if something else piqued my interest while reading, I had to go through the same process to look that up, too. As a book lover, I must admit I feel a bit of nostalgia for those days even as the internet has revolutionized how I search for information. But, it's also amazing how we can click on a hyperlink to find related information without flipping pages or getting out another book.

Within our Bibles, many versions include footnotes or even a concordance to help us see links between different passages. Before the printing press made paper Bibles an option, written communication looked much different. While most of us have likely seen a picture of a scroll, if not a real scroll in a museum, it can be hard to grasp how different the experience of reading from one would have been from what we're used to today.

And so, I found it fascinating when I heard Dr. Tim Mackie from The Bible Project describe how the biblical authors created their own hyperlinks of sorts by carefully choosing words. For example, throughout the Scriptures we see repeated words, themes, and places the authors used to connect different texts almost as if they had the blue underlined words we're so familiar with now.[vi]

Over the coming weeks, we'll see some of those connections between the prophetic books and other parts of the Bible. And one theme we'll see woven throughout reminds me of the truth of Romans 3:23 where it says,

"There is no distinction, for all have sinned and fall short of the glory of God."

But we'll also see how despite human failings, God continued to love His people. Out of that love, God made several covenants: first with Noah, then Abraham, next with all the Israelites led by Moses, and later with King David. Yesterday the covenant referenced in the warning part of the prophetic message referred to the Mosaic covenant. The people continually broke their side of it and the prophets called them to repent and change their ways or be punished. Because we'll see references, links, back to that Mosaic covenant, we're going to take a quick look at when it got established.

Read Exodus 34:1-14. Did you notice any repetition or references that may have been intended to remind you of something (such as in verses 1 and 4)?

What aspects of the LORD's character do you see in this passage?

The reference to chiseling "two stone tablets like the first ones" should either have been a reminder or a clue that something significant had happened before this related to the original tablets. And indeed, Exodus 31:18-33:23 tell how God had given Moses the original tablets inscribed with the terms of the covenant, followed by how the Israelites had made a golden calf to worship while Moses was gone. When Moses saw what the Israelites were doing, he became very angry and threw down the two tablets, smashing them.

After Moses dealt with the people and interceded with the LORD to keep Him from destroying the Israelites, we come to Exodus 34. As the LORD gave Moses a new copy of the covenant, God tells Moses His name, Yahweh, the LORD. You'll see those names used in the rest of this study since the prophets all tie back to this covenant. The prophets will also refer to the description in this passage of Yahweh's character. If you continue reading in Exodus 34, it's clear the people must not worship any other gods.

Now, read Deuteronomy 10:12-22. Who does this passage say that God loves (v. 15 & 18)?

This passage tells us God is higher than any other gods or lords. He is mighty, awesome, and merciful. He is just toward widows and orphans and a provider to foreigners. We see that Yahweh specifically chose to love the family of Israel. Yet, verse 18 also says He loves the foreigners living among the Israelites.

In light of God's love for both the Israelites and non-Israelites living among them, what does God tell the people to do?

The people are to love, fear and obey Yahweh. And then Moses wrote that the Israelites, too, should love foreigners, before going back to the theme that the people should fear, worship and obey God. As we'll see, these themes of loving God and loving others will come up again and again in the prophets.

As we wrap up for today, think about how this still applies to our lives today. If you had to rate yourself on a scale of 1-10 with 10 being the best, how would you rate yourself at loving and obeying God? And how would you rate yourself at loving others?

<u>Loving God</u>   <u>Loving Others</u>

1 2 3 4 5 6 7 8 9 10   1 2 3 4 5 6 7 8 9 10

Why did you choose those numbers? Where do you think you could use improvement and why? Or what do you need to do to maintain where you are?

PRAYER FOCUS

Reflecting on the numbers you chose above, ask God to show you any areas of your life He wants you to notice. Are there ways your heart may need reoriented to love God first? And does anyone, even a whole group, come to mind as someone you struggle to love? Ask Him to open your eyes to any changes He may be asking you to make.

THE GREATEST COMMANDMENTS

"Jesus replied, "'You must love the LORD your God with all your heart, all your soul, and all your mind.' This is the first and greatest commandment. A second is equally important: 'Love your neighbor as yourself.' The entire law and all the demands of the prophets are based on these two commandments.'"
– Matthew 22:37-40

My daughters have good memories, especially about certain topics. It's not uncommon for them to say something like, "Mom, you said I can have a popsicle!" and I have to recall whether I did in fact make that commitment. Other requests, though, hardly need asked or at the least, don't require much thought on my part. More green beans? Absolutely! A bedtime story and prayers together before bed? Yes, of course!

The heart behind the commandments God gave the Israelites through Moses was similar—so engrained throughout that it should have been as simple to remember as a bedtime routine. As Jesus said in the passage above from Matthew, the whole law and the prophets were based on loving God first and then loving our neighbor.

If you're thinking that seems overly simple, it's important to know the order of the Hebrew Bible at that time wasn't quite the same as what we have in the Old Testament. It's not clear when the order changed, but during Jesus' ministry, there were three sections that would have been written on multiple scrolls, as in the table on the next page.

SECTIONS OF THE HEBREW BIBLE

Torah*	Nevi'im (The Prophets)	Kethuvim (The Writings)
1. Genesis 2. Exodus 3. Leviticus 4. Numbers 5. Deuteronomy	*Early Prophets*: 1. Joshua 2. Judges 3. Samuel 4. Kings *Later Prophets*: 1. Isaiah 2. Jeremiah 3. Ezekiel 4. the Twelve: Hosea, Joel, Amos, Obadiah, Jonah, Micah, Nahum, Habakkuk, Zephaniah, Haggai, Zechariah, Malachi**	1. Psalms 2. Job 3. Proverbs 4. Ruth 5. Song of Songs*** 6. Ecclesiastes 7. Lamentations 8. Esther 9. Daniel**** 10. Ezra-Nehemiah 11. Chronicles[vii]
Note: The Torah is often translated as "law" because this is how it was translated from Hebrew to Greek in the centuries just before Jesus' birth. This Greek translation was called the Septuagint and you may see it footnoted in your Bible today.[viii] A more literal translation of Torah from Hebrew to English would be "teaching"[ix] or "instruction"[x].	**Note:* These 12 were often referred to as Shneim'Asar (the Twelve) and written on one scroll.[xi] Today, many scholars refer to them as The Book of the Twelve.[xii]	***Note:* Some versions call this book Song of Solomon. ****Note:* The book of Daniel is here in the Writings as wisdom literature rather than with the prophets. I've included it in this study, though, since it's placed with the prophetic books in our Old Testament order.

So, when Jesus says the two commandments to love God and our neighbors underpin the law and the prophets, He's saying it underpins *all* the books listed in those two groups above.

Did you know before that the order of the Old Testament books today isn't the same as what it used to be? Can you think of any ways that changing the order may be significant?

If you look closely, you will see connections between the original three sections of the Old Testament we may miss in their current order. However, as we look for those connections, they're still there—just not as obvious as if the order matched the Hebrew Bible.

One example is how we may miss what Jesus meant when He referred to the law and the prophets, not realizing He was referring to whole sections of the Old Testament. Another is how both the Torah and Prophets sections of the Hebrew Bible have similar themes in their final words.[xiii] To provide some context in Deuteronomy though, we'll also look back at the passage in chapter 18 that we read two days ago.

> **Read these passages:**
> o **Deuteronomy 18:15-19**
> o **Deuteronomy 34:10-12**
> o **Malachi 4:4-6**

> What do both Deuteronomy and Malachi leave us waiting for? If you're familiar with the story of Jesus, how does Jesus complete this?

At the end of Deuteronomy, we find the people of Israel poised to enter the Promised Land after 40 years in the wilderness where God gave them his teaching/instruction. During Moses' lifetime, Deuteronomy 18:15-19 tells us God would raise up another prophet like Moses. Yet, the closing to the Torah in Deuteronomy 34:10 says: *"There has never been another prophet in Israel like Moses, whom the LORD knew face to face."* Those words were written after Moses' death and seem to still anticipate the coming of another prophet just like God had promised Moses during his lifetime.[xiv]

Then, the final words in Malachi, currently the last book of our Old Testament, but also the final book in the Hebrew Nevi'im, Prophets section, includes a promise that a prophet like Elijah is coming. Despite the many prophets in the Old Testament, including Elijah, it closes still looking for someone else. So, like the Torah, the Prophets section also ended with a promise that there would be someone coming to turn people to the LORD.

Circling back to Jesus saying the whole law and prophets are based on the commands to love God and to love our neighbors, let's look at what God wrote on the tablets He gave Moses when He made the covenant with Israel.

Read Deuteronomy 5:1-22. See if you can categorize the Ten Commandments you just read into groups based on the two commands Jesus said are the greatest.

Loving God   *Loving Others*

The first four commandments all relate to loving God with our heart, soul and mind, while the final six all tie to loving our neighbor as ourselves. If you go through the other commands in the Torah, you'll see how they tie back to one of those two commandments as well. We'll start seeing the same connection to the prophets over the coming weeks as they point back to these commands as well.

Does seeing that Jesus said the basis for the prophets' message came down to loving God and loving your neighbor impact how you think about the prophetic books? Why or why not?

Thinking about any times you've read in the prophetic books before, how would you have described them? If you haven't spent much time reading them before, what has kept you from studying them? What do you hope to gain from studying them now?

PRAYER FOCUS

Thinking about the order of the Bible might be a new thought for you. As we continue to set the stage for studying the prophets, ask the LORD to open your eyes to new insights He may have for you over the coming weeks.

DAY 4

EYES THAT SEE, EARS THAT HEAR

"And He said, 'Yes, go, and say to this people,

'Listen carefully, but do not understand.
Watch closely, but learn nothing.'
Harden the hearts of these people.
Plug their ears and shut their eyes.
That way, they will not see with their eyes,
nor hear with their ears,
nor understand with their hearts
and turn to me for healing."
– Isaiah 6:9-10

Yesterday a friend asked if I had any new books to recommend. She knows I read a lot and always have at least a few books going at once. I read many genres, but one style you won't typically find in my stack is poetry. It's not so much that I don't like a good poem; it's just not my go-to style. And if I'm going to read poetry, I usually stick to the type that rhymes.

You may recall from Day 1 of this study that about a third of the Bible is actually poetry.

> While one book of the Bible isn't necessarily written in only one style, what book(s) come to your mind as being poetry?

Out of curiosity, I asked that same question to some family and friends. The hands down favorite was Psalms with nearly everyone listing that first. Second place had an even tie with 60 percent saying Proverbs and Song of Songs (Solomon), although the same people didn't necessarily pick both. Ecclesiastes came in next with 40 percent of the vote. The final two were Job and Lamentations which both got one mention, although not by the same person. Some noted that the books they listed weren't all poetry, too, acknowledging the style can vary within one book.

No one picked any of the prophetic books, although the prophet Jeremiah wrote Lamentations. Would you be surprised to know that a poetic style is very common in the prophets, though? That may leave you wondering, *what exactly makes something poetry*?!

Jot down any words that come to mind that you would use to describe poetry.

Chances are you mentioned at least a couple of these descriptions: rhyme, rhythm, sound, meter, repetition, descriptive language, stanzas, lines, and/or figures of speech.[xv] It can be easy to see how these descriptions could apply to many of the Psalms. We're less likely to have noticed these in the books of the prophets, but the way passages are printed on the page can give you a clue when you get to poetry.

Look back at the verses from Isaiah 6 at the beginning of today's lesson. What stands out to you about the formatting?

Notice how most of the passage is written in stanzas rather than paragraph form? And now think about the content. Will the people's hearts *literally* be hardened, their ears plugged, and their eyes shut? No, the passage clearly refers to the people's ability to understand God's truths in their minds and hearts in order to repent from their sins. This is a spiritual hardening of their hearts, not physical. The passage uses poetic imagery to give us a visual picture of what the author meant.

Bible scholar and teacher, J. Daniel Hays, says, "the primary characteristics of Hebrew poetry are (1) density (succinctness), (2) parallelism, (3) figurative imagery, and (4) high concentration of wordplay."[xvi] He also notes that while the prophetic books include a variety of literary styles, many include some or all of those characteristics making them very poetic.[xvii] We'll unpack each of those a little.

Density: This speaks for itself. You'll see a lot of condensed ideas in the books of the prophets. They minimize the number of words used and the words used were carefully chosen.[xviii]

Parallelism: Biblical poetry often has stanzas with two lines where the second reiterates the same idea as the first, contrasts the first line, or adds to the first line.[xix] Here are some examples of each:

Reference	Verse	Type of Parallelism[xx]
Isaiah 54:4a	*"Fear not; you will no longer live in shame.*	Line 1
	Don't be afraid; there is no more disgrace for you."	Same as line 1
Isaiah 54:7	*"For a brief moment I abandoned you,*	Line 1
	but with great compassion I will take you back."	Contrast to line 1
Isaiah 54:9	*"Just as I swore in the time of Noah that I would never again let a flood cover the earth*	Line 1
	so now I swear that I will never again be angry and punish you."	Addition to line 1

Stanzas can also parallel other stanzas over more than two lines.[xxi] Because of how parallel ideas are presented, you'll see a lot of repetition in biblical poetry. You'll also see names and places intended to remind you of something you've read before like we talked about on Day 2. If we don't recognize the name/place and don't stop to look up the connection, we can lose some of the significance of *why* it's mentioned. I'll point some of these out as we go and hopefully even more will stand out to you.

Figurative Imagery: You may not have thought about figurative language much since Language Arts class, but chances are some of the more common types found in poetry will sound familiar to you. Just for fun, see if you can match the following verses and figures of speech.[xxii] It may help to read the verses in context. Answers are on page 26 although some could contain more than one type.

____ 1. Ezekiel 20:39a – *"As for you, O people of Israel, this is what the Sovereign LORD says: Go right ahead and worship your idols..."*

a. Simile (comparison using like or as)

____ 2. Joel 2:11a – *"The LORD is at the head of the column. He leads them with a shout. This is His mighty army, and they follow His orders."*

b. Metaphor (comparison without like or as)

____ 3. Isaiah 5:4 – *"What more could I have done for my vineyard that I have not already done? When I expected sweet grapes, why did my vineyard give me bitter grapes?"*

c. Hypocatastasis (indirect analogy)

____ 4. Amos 4:6 – *"I brought hunger to every city and famine to every town. But still you would not return to me," says the LORD."*

d. Hyperbole (conscious exaggeration for the sake of effect)

____ 5. Micah 1:4 – *"The mountains melt beneath his feet and flow into the valleys like wax in a fire, like water pouring down a hill."*

e. Personification (giving human features to nonhuman things)

____ 6. Isaiah 55:12b – *"The mountains and hills will burst into song, and the trees of the field will clap their hands!"*

f. Anthropomorphism (giving human features to God)

____ 7. Zechariah 9:13a – *"Judah is my bow, and Israel is my arrow. Jerusalem is my sword..."*

g. Metonym (stating a cause so the reader infers effect or vice versa)

____ 8. Jeremiah 9:1a – *"If only my head were a pool of water and my eyes a fountain of tears."*

h. Irony/Sarcasm (saying the opposite of what is really meant)

Wordplay: Those of us who can't read Hebrew will likely miss this, but the prophets often play with words, choosing them carefully in the original language. [xxiii] For example, a particular word may have been chosen in Hebrew because it sounds like another word. The original audience would have caught the similarity, but we lose that in translation.[xxiv] And there are certainly times when even scholars disagree about the intended meaning of a particular word or phrase. We're fortunate to have Bibles today with footnotes that may point out original word meaning, and Bible Hub offers free online resources for this, too. (See https://biblehub.com.)

> Do you find the style of the prophetic books easy or difficult to read, or something in between? Has the writing style impacted any previous attempts you've made to study these books? If so, in what way?

PRAYER FOCUS

Today has been heavy on literary features we'll refer back to in the coming weeks. As we close, spend time in prayer asking God to give you eyes to see and ears to hear as we move through the coming weeks of study.

Answer Key
1 (h); 2 (f); 3 (c); 4 (g); 5 (a); 6 (e); 7 (b); 8 (d)

MOVING PIECES

"Praise the name of God forever and ever,
*   for He has all wisdom and power.*
He controls the course of world events;
*   He removes kings and sets up other kings.*
He gives wisdom to the wise
*   and knowledge to the scholars.*
He reveals deep and mysterious things
*   and knows what lies hidden in darkness,*
*   though He is surrounded by light."*
– Daniel 2:20b-22

This week, we've been setting the stage for what we're going to read over the next five sessions. We've seen the Cliffs Notes version of the message of the prophets—that the people had broken Yahweh's covenant, would face judgment if they didn't repent, but ultimately were still offered hope of restoration. We've looked at the covenant God made with the Israelites and how the twin commands to love God and love our neighbors undergirds them. Then yesterday we took a crash course in the poetic literary style often found in the prophets.

We haven't yet looked at where these books fit in the geopolitical climate of their day, which forms another critical component of understanding them. To provide more context, the rest of this study is grouped loosely by the dominant empires when these prophets lived. They also lived during the time after Israel had split into two nations, Israel to the north and Judah to the south. We'll read highlights about some of the kings of Israel and Judah in the books of Kings and Chronicles as it helps paint a picture of the state of affairs during the prophets' ministries.

To start getting a sense for where the books we're going to study fit historically, we're going to read some verses that introduce each one. Use the general timeline on the next page to see where these prophets fit; some are harder to place. The kings in the timeline with their names italicized followed the LORD—none of the kings of Israel received this distinction.

CONDENSED TIMELINE

Empire →	Assyria						Babylon	Persia
Kings of Israel	Jeroboam II	Zechariah / Shallum / Menahem / Pekahiah	Pekah / Hoshea	Fall of Thebes	Fall of Nineveh		Fall of Jerusalem	Fall of Babylon / Cyrus / Darius
Kings of Judah	Uzziah	Jotham	Ahaz	Hezekiah	Manasseh	Amon / Josiah	Jehoahaz / Jehoiakim	Jehoiachin / Zedekiah

As you read the next set of passages, highlight the names of kings and put a tally mark next to their names in the timeline.

- **Isaiah 1:1** – "*These are the visions that Isaiah son of Amoz saw concerning Judah and Jerusalem. He saw these visions during the years when Uzziah, Jotham, Ahaz, and Hezekiah were kings of Judah.*"
- **Hosea 1:1** – "*The LORD gave this message to Hosea son of Beeri during the years when Uzziah, Jotham, Ahaz, and Hezekiah were kings of Judah, and Jeroboam son of Jehoash was king of Israel.*"
- **Amos 1:1** – "*This message was given to Amos, a shepherd from the town of Tekoa in Judah. He received this message in visions two years before the earthquake, when Uzziah was king of Judah and Jeroboam II, the son of Jehoash, was king of Israel.*"
- **Jonah 1:1-2; 2 Kings 14:25** – "*The LORD gave this message to Jonah son of Amittai: "Get up and go to the great city of Nineveh. Announce my judgment against it because I have seen how wicked its people are." (2 Kings 14:25) "[King] Jeroboam II recovered the territories of Israel between Lebo-hamath and the Dead Sea, just as the LORD had promised through Jonah son of Amittai, the prophet from Gath-hepher.*"
- **Micah 1:1** – "*The LORD gave this message to Micah of Moresheth during the years when Jotham, Ahaz, and Hezekiah were kings of Judah. The visions he saw concerned both Samaria and Jerusalem.*

What stands out to you in these brief intros? Can you tell where these prophets lived in relation to each other? Can you tell if they from Israel or Judah?

Isaiah, Amos and Micah were from Judah, although for Micah you would have had to look up the location of Moresheth to know that.[xxv] Jonah was from Israel and while it's not explicitly stated, the book of Hosea seems as though he was from Israel also.

As you read these next verses, circle the verbs Nahum used regarding Nineveh and Thebes.

- **Nahum 1:1; 3:1a, 3:8a, 3:10a** – *"This message concerning Nineveh came as a vision to Nahum, who lived in Elkosh." (3:1a) "What sorrow awaits Nineveh, the city of murder and lies!" (3:8a) "Are you any better than the city of Thebes, situated on the Nile River, surrounded by water?" (3:10a) "Yet Thebes fell, and her people were led away as captives."*

Look at the timeline on the previous page. Can you tell where Nahum fits based on the verb tenses he used to talk about those cities?

The timeline doesn't include dates, but Manasseh was king for 55 years while his son Amon only reigned for 2. That makes it more likely Nahum prophesied during Manasseh's much longer reign, but the text doesn't say for sure.

As you read the next set of passages, highlight the names of kings and put a tally mark next to their names in the timeline.

- **Jeremiah 1:1-3** – *"These are the words of Jeremiah son of Hilkiah, one of the priests from the town of Anathoth in the land of Benjamin. The LORD gave messages to Jeremiah during the thirteenth year of the reign of Josiah son of Amon, king of Judah. The LORD's messages continued throughout the reign of King Jehoiakim, Josiah's son, until the eleventh year of the reign of King Zedekiah, another of Josiah's sons. In August of that eleventh year the people of Jerusalem were taken away as captives."*
- **Zephaniah 1:1** – *"The LORD gave this message to Zephaniah when Josiah son of Amon was king of Judah. Zephaniah was the son of Cushi, son of Gedaliah, son of Amariah, son of Hezekiah."*
- **Daniel 1:1, 1:3, 1:6, 1:21** – *"During the third year of King Jehoiakim's reign in Judah, King Nebuchadnezzar of Babylon came to Jerusalem and besieged it." (1:3) "Then the king ordered Ashpenaz, his chief of staff, to bring to the palace some of the young men of Judah's royal family and other noble families, who had been brought to Babylon as captives." (1:6) "Daniel, Hananiah, Mishael, and Azariah were four of the young men*

chosen, all from the tribe of Judah." (1:21) "*Daniel remained in the royal service until the first year of the reign of King Cyrus.*"

- **Ezekiel 1:1-3** – "*On July 31 of my thirtieth year, while I was with the Judean exiles beside the Kebar River in Babylon, the heavens were opened and I saw visions of God. This happened during the fifth year of King Jehoiachin's captivity. (The LORD gave this message to Ezekiel son of Buzi, a priest, beside the Kebar River in the land of the Babylonians, and he felt the hand of the LORD take hold of him.)*"

What stands out to you in these brief intros? Can you tell where these four men lived and whether they overlapped with each other?

Zephaniah and Jeremiah both prophesied during King Josiah's reign. Jeremiah continued on and overlapped with both Daniel and Ezekiel. Daniel and Ezekiel were exiled from Judah to Babylon. While Ezekiel mentioned Jehoiachin's name, it says he was in captivity so we can infer Zedekiah was actually king when Ezekiel's ministry began.

As you read the next set of passages, highlight the names of places.

- **Habakkuk 1:1; 1:6** – "*This is the message that the prophet Habakkuk received in a vision.*" (1:6) "*I am raising up the Babylonians, a cruel and violent people. They will march across the world and conquer other lands.*"
- **Obadiah 1:1, 1:10-11a, 12b** – "*This is the vision that the Sovereign LORD revealed to Obadiah concerning the land of Edom.*" (1:10-11a) "*Because of the violence you did to your close relatives in Israel, you will be filed with shame and destroyed forever. When they were invaded you stood aloof, refusing to help them.*" (1:12b) "*You should not have rejoiced when the people of Judah suffered such misfortune. You should not have spoken arrogantly in that terrible time of trouble.*"
- **Joel 1:1, 2:1a** – "*The LORD gave this message to Joel son of Pethuel.*" (2:1a) "*Sound the alarm in Jerusalem! Raise the battle cry on my holy mountain!*"

Can you tell how these three prophets fit in history? (If not you're in good company!)

As you read this final set of passages, underline the dates/years and circle the names of places. Put a tally mark next to king's names in the timeline.

- **Haggai 1:1** – "*On August 29 of the second year of King Darius's reign, the LORD gave a message through the prophet Haggai to Zerubbabel son of Shealtiel, governor of Judah, and to Jeshua son of Jehozadak, the high priest.*"
- **Zechariah 1:1** – "*In November of the second year of King Darius's reign, the LORD gave this message to the prophet Zechariah son of Berekiah and grandson of Iddo.*"
- **Malachi 1:1, 1:3-4a** – "*This is the message that the LORD gave to Israel through the prophet Malachi.*" (1:3-4a) "*but I rejected his brother, Esau, and devastated his hill country. I turned Esau's inheritance into a desert for jackals. Esau's descendants in Edom may say, "We have been shattered, but we will rebuild the ruins." But the LORD of Heaven's Armies replies, "They may try to rebuild, but I will demolish them again."*"

Can you tell where these prophets fit in the timeline?

Haggai and Zechariah give very specific dates for when their ministries began. Malachi is less clear, although scholars estimate it was written around 450 BC.[xxvi]

Look back at the timeline. Are there any kings that you didn't put a tally mark by? Do you have any guess as to why those kings weren't included?

Only one of the kings of Israel got mentioned. Israel experienced turmoil after King Jeroboam II and the kings that followed him were weak. This may be why the prophets omit them while naming Judah's kings from the same time period as the Israelite ones he doesn't mention.[xxvii]

Two of the final kings of Judah who don't get mentioned, except where Ezekiel references Jehoiachin's captivity, both reigned for only three months each.[xxviii] And while I mentioned Nahum likely lived during Manasseh's reign, we'll talk later about why there seems to be a gap in the prophets during that time period.

Using the kings mentioned in many of the books and other markers, we can place most of the prophets in the general time when their ministry took place. If you flip to the timeline at the back of this book on page 150, you'll see a general idea of how they correlate to each other as well as to the kings of Israel and Judah plus the dominant empires. I've marked a couple with a question mark where it's harder to tell.

Geographically, Israel and Judah were periodically located in the middle of conflict between Egypt to the south and Assyria or Babylon to the north. Other surrounding countries played a role as well, including Edom and Moab. You'll see references to these nations and a few others in the prophetic books. For the most part though, we'll spend more time looking at prophecies to Israel and Judah.

Because we're far removed from these times and places, it's easy to look at the names of these countries and time periods and start zoning out. Yet, we've likely seen similar international tensions in our modern era that might help us contextualize the setting for our study.

> Thinking about our world today, in the ovals below jot down the names of countries that stand out to you as regional or world powers in some way. You can add more ovals as needed. Off to the side, jot down the names of any countries they have been in conflict with in recent decades if not already listed in a circle. Draw lines between the countries that have had conflict with each other.

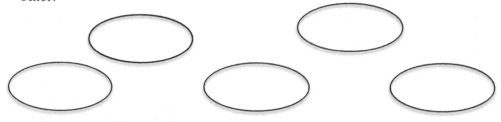

> As you think of the countries you jotted down, did you start feeling any emotions tied to any of them? (For example, pride, loyalty, anger, fear, concern, doubt, frustration, powerlessness, envy, sadness, or even bitterness?) If so, why?

In a similar way, the prophets and people who lived during their lifetimes would have had some strong emotions when they thought about Israel, Judah, Assyria, Babylon, and/or Persia depending on when and where they lived. Keeping that in mind and even imagining your own country in place of one of these over the next few weeks can help give a little perspective on their viewpoint going forward.

Have you read any of the prophetic books while also looking at other parts of the Old Testament from the same time period? How do you think understanding what was happening in Israel and Judah, as well as between other nations in the region, might help with understanding the prophets?

What do you hope to learn or see over the rest of the study?

PRAYER FOCUS

As we close today, spend time in prayer asking God to open your eyes to what He may be doing in your life. Praise Him for what you see Him doing in your life and surrender any areas you may need to release.

Before getting together, have everyone complete Session 1.

1.   Open in prayer.

2.   Feel free to use the following questions with your group. You can also ask people to share what stood out to them each day.

- What do you hope to get out of this study?

- When you hear the word "prophet", what comes to mind? Why?

- Do you think God still sends prophets today and if so, how could we recognize them?

- What stood out to you the most about the link between the covenant God gave Moses and the prophets?

- Had you thought about the order of the Bible before?

- Thinking about anything you already know about the book of Daniel, can you see any reason the original Hebrew order placed it with the wisdom books instead of with the Nevi'im (Prophets)?

- Were you surprised so much of the Bible is written in poetry? What challenges do you think people may have with understanding biblical poetry?

- How do you think understanding the geopolitical context of the prophetic books could enhance your reading of them?

- What questions do you have?

Assyrian Dominance

SESSION 2
THE HEART OF THE MATTER

DAY 1
NO OTHER GODS

"I will rescue you for my sake—
yes, for My own sake!
I will not let my reputation be tarnished,
I will not share my glory with idols!"
– Isaiah 48:11

Remember last session when we read Matthew 22:37-40? That's where Jesus said the greatest commandment was to "love the LORD your God with all your heart, all your soul, and all your mind". It sounds so simple, but as we see throughout the pages of the Old Testament, the Israelites kept turning to idol worship instead.

Isaiah 48:11 tells us, God will not share His glory with idols. While He offers opportunities for heart change, He will ultimately punish those who worship something other than Himself. Over these next two sessions as we look at the prophets who lived during the time when the Assyrian Empire was dominant, we'll see a repeated call to worship God alone.

Hosea was one of the prophets God used to warn the people of Israel to repent and turn back to God. Hosea 1-3 describes how the LORD asked Hosea to do something very unexpected in his personal life. As a quick summary, Hosea 1:2 says,

> *"When the LORD first began speaking to Israel through Hosea, he said to him, "Go and marry a prostitute, so that some of her children will be conceived in prostitution. This will illustrate how Israel has acted like a prostitute by turning against the LORD and worshiping other gods."*

They had several children, but then she apparently left Hosea and went back to prostitution. At some point, God told him to go bring her back as his wife, which Hosea did at a cost. Can you imagine what Hosea would have felt?!

With that background in mind, **read Hosea 4**. What sin(s) did Hosea identify and who committed them?

Did you recognize many of the Ten Commandments in that list? The Israelites and even their priests were guilty of sinning against the LORD and others. They failed to truly love God and certainly not their neighbors.

What imagery does Hosea use to describe Israel and its relationship with God? How does that relate to what God asked Hosea to do in his personal life?

Hosea called Israel a prostitute for turning to idols in place of worshiping the LORD. This would have had a deeply personal meaning for Hosea. His own experience of being abandoned by someone he loved intimately likely impacted how he shared God's messages with the people.

Look back at verse 15. What do you notice about Israel's sin compared to Judah?

As the chapter concludes, do you see any hope for Israel? **Yes No**
Why or why not?

Hosea had a more favorable estimation of Judah here, but his message to Israel has warnings of judgment without hope for restoration. Skipping ahead a little, we're going to compare and contrast another chapter with what we just read.

Read Hosea 11. Did you recognize the names in verse 8, Admah and Zeboiim?
Yes No

This is an example of place names as links to an earlier part of the Bible. If you didn't recognize them, you can follow the links by reading Genesis 14:8, 18:20-21 and 19:24-25. And if none of those passages sounds familiar, you may also want to read Genesis 18:16-19:29. I remember the story of Sodom and Gomorrah, but somehow missed that they weren't the only cities God destroyed in Genesis 19. We'll come back to this in a little bit.

What similar themes do you see in Hosea 11 that were also in Hosea 4?

At the same time, did you notice a major difference between the two chapters? In what way does chapter 11 complete the 3-part prophetic message from Session 1 (warning to repent, judgment for failure to repent, and yet, hope)?

We still see the indictment against Israel for turning to idolatry. God says the people don't truly honor Him even when they say they do. Here again, we see that Israel will be punished for the people's sins. We also see a contrast at the end between Israel's deceit and Judah's obedience just as it said in chapter 4.

Both chapters 4 and 11 have warnings that the people had turned away from God (part 1) and a promise that they would experience punishment as a result (part 2). While chapter 4 stopped there, Hosea 11:8-11 adds the third part—**hope**. Despite their sin, He was still willing to restore them if they would turn back to Him. And to contrast this, He reminded them of the ruined cities of Admah and Zeboiim. He had destroyed those cities along with their neighbors because of their wickedness and Israel was headed down the same path. Yet, God longed to show them compassion instead.

Even with the judgment the people deserved, we see God's character shining through. The people were faithless, but God remained faithful to them. He offered them mercy and forgiveness, demonstrating unconditional love, unmerited favor. (Remember how Yahweh described Himself in Exodus 34?)

> Instead of using the imagery of a prostitute/unfaithful wife, what relationship does Hosea use in chapter 11 to illustrate His relationship with Israel?

In spite of Israel's ongoing disregard for God, He still loved them. The father/son imagery in chapter 11 puts that love a little more in perspective. It might be hard to love an unfaithful spouse but seeing the unrepentant one as your child makes it easier to understand Yahweh's compassion and love for His unworthy people.

That same unchanging love explains why God loved *us* so much that He sent Jesus. (See John 3:16-21.) Matthew 2:15 in the account of how Mary and Joseph took baby Jesus to live in Egypt even points back to the prophecy in Hosea 11:1 that God would call His Son out of Egypt.[i] And with the people's obvious inability to keep their end of Yahweh's covenant, we again see why He sent Jesus to make a way for us to be restored into relationship with God. His love toward us remains today even though we're no more capable of keeping the LORD's covenant through Moses than the Israelites were thousands of years ago.

Applying this to your own life, how have you looked to other things instead of to God? What changes may you need to make?

Yet, where you have seen God's unmerited love and favor in your life in spite of how you may have strayed from His path?

PRAYER FOCUS

As we close today, spend time thanking God for His love for you. At the same time, ask Him to open your eyes to any ways you may have allowed other things to take His place in your heart (i.e. money, success, relationships, etc.). No matter what He may show you, you can rest assured His love for you hasn't changed.

WHO DO YOU SAY I AM?

"Then he [Jesus] asked them, 'But who do you say I am?' Simon Peter answered,
'You are the Messiah, the Son of the living God.' Jesus replied, 'You are blessed,
Simon son of John, because my Father in heaven has revealed this to you. You did
not learn this from any human being.'"
– Matthew 16:15-17

I love how God gives each of us different talents and abilities. Of course, how we use them can vary based on where we live, how we're raised, or the events going on in our lifetimes. Two people with similar aptitudes might accomplish very different things, or people with opposite backgrounds might end up in the same career.

We see the latter dynamic with several of the prophets God sent to Israel around the same time. Yesterday we read from Hosea and the main info we have about him has to do with his family, including his dad, circumstances of his marriage, and his children's names. Today, we're going to look at one of his counterparts, Amos, a farmer/rancher who owned sheep and grew sycamore figs.[ii]

Amos lived and farmed in Judah, but God called him to speak to the people of Israel. So, he left his land to go as a missionary to the country next door. Because Israel and Judah had once been the same nation, they likely shared a lot of similar customs besides speaking the same language.

The opening verse tells us this message came to Amos "two years before the earthquake" while King Jeroboam II reigned in Israel and King Uzziah in Judah. This specific reference leads scholars to believe Amos' ministry took place over a short time, possibly only a few months.[iii] While earthquakes happen fairly often in that region, the way Amos 1:1 calls this "the earthquake" suggests it was a particularly large one. Zechariah 14:5 refers to "the earthquake in the days of Uzziah king of Judah" that made people flee and archeological evidence from Hazor in what was northern Israel shows evidence "that a sizable earthquake occurred around 760 BC".[iv] We don't know for sure whether that was the same one Amos referenced, but the timing fits.

All that to say: God gave Amos a specific task at a certain time and while it didn't align with his occupation, he obeyed. We have no indication he wanted to go to

Israel, but just as Hosea obeyed God's call to marry a prostitute, Amos left his farm and flocks to go speak the LORD's message to his northern neighbors.

Read Amos 4. Which parts of the prophetic message do you see in this chapter?
- ☐ Warning of how the people had sinned
- ☐ Pronouncements of judgment for sin
- ☐ Hope of restoration with God

While we see lots of warnings about sin and the consequences the people would face, we don't see the third part of the prophetic message here—hope. And sadly, the judgment Amos warned about in verses 2-3 happened in 722 BC when Assyria conquered Israel maybe 40 years after these prophecies.[v]

What do you notice about Amos' literary style compared to what we've already studied?

We see poetic stanzas again here, and Amos uses a lot of visual imagery. Can you imagine how the Israelite women would have felt when he called them "fat cows"? He certainly would have gotten their attention, but heart change may have been another matter.

What sins does Amos call out in verses 1 and 5? How does this give you a glimpse into how the people he was speaking to lived?

We start seeing a picture of how the people Amos addressed were wealthy, prideful and self-important. He used harsh language to describe how they had mistreated the poor and needy. Again, this lack of love for their neighbors showed their breach of Yahweh's covenant.

What do verses 4-5 tell us about the people's religious practices?

As Amos continued to paint a picture of what the people were like, he sarcastically told them to continue their idolatry and disobedience to Yahweh. Yet, he also noted they still offered daily sacrifices, tithed every three days and brought thanksgiving and voluntary offerings to the LORD. While that might sound like good things, he followed it by accusing them of doing this just so they could brag about it.

Verses 7-11 show how God tried to get their attention through one calamity after another, but the repeated line after each one tells us the people never returned to God. (Did you notice the reference to Sodom and Gomorrah, too?) Through each one, the LORD wanted their hearts to turn back to Him, but nothing had worked so Amos promised the people Yahweh was about to bring disaster on them in judgment for their sins.

Why do you think Amos ended his message with verse 13 the way he did?

Amos pointed them back to who Yahweh is. We see similar descriptions in multiple places in the Old Testament.[vi] This wasn't just a message from a Judean farmer, but from the LORD God of Heaven's Armies.

It reminds me of how fourteen years ago, God began taking me on a journey of really knowing WHO He is—taking *head* knowledge of His character and turning it into *heart* knowledge. To be honest, I was confused at first because I had grown up in church and knew all the "right" Sunday School answers. I couldn't see why God was taking me back to what at first seemed like such basic concepts.

As the LORD reminded me over and over that He is faithful, I felt a bit hurt because I knew God was faithful! But as He kept showing me His faithfulness through the pages of Scripture and through all He did in my life during that season, it slowly dawned on me I hadn't been living like I really, truly **believed** He was faithful.

When I reached the point where I knew that I knew *that I knew* that God is indeed faithful, He began focusing me on understanding that He is love. Again, my first thought was—of course I know You're love! Yet again, as the months went by, He showed me repeatedly I had not been living like I really believed that not only does God love me, but that God Himself *is* love. As He opened my eyes to what that really meant, it shifted my heart and the way I saw both others and myself in a powerful way.

This pattern continued for several years where God embedded truths about His character into my heart, one by one. While it may sound easy, it was much harder to learn than I could ever have imagined. I had some deeply embedded wrong views of God that needed uprooted first. But on the other side, I emerged with a bedrock solid understanding of who God truly is that can never be taken from me. When something hard crosses my path or I have things I don't understand going on in my life, God always takes me back to that knowledge of His character. While it doesn't fix external circumstances, it always brings my heart back to a place of peace even in the turmoil life can bring.

And so as we close today, my question for you goes back to what Jesus asked His disciples in Matthew 16:15:

Who do you truly believe that God is?

If you were to list out His attributes and characteristics, what would you write and do you really *believe* they are true?

Like my initial response to God back in 2007, you may read this thinking—yes, of course I know who God is and believe! But I'd challenge you to spend some time praying and asking God to reveal to you whether you have areas of your heart where you *don't* really believe He is who He says He is. Where you don't really believe He is faithful, or loving, or a provider, or gracious, or any other number of descriptions you could list off from your head knowledge. It can be a much harder question to answer than it might sound!

PRAYER FOCUS

As you reflect on your own heart and your beliefs about God, take some time to pray as you feel led. At the same time, I'm praying the words of Ephesians 1:17-20 over you,

> *"Asking God, the glorious Father of our Lord Jesus Christ, to give you spiritual wisdom and insight so that you might grow in your knowledge of God. I pray that your hearts will be flooded with light so that you can understand the confident hope He has given to those He called—His holy people who are His rich and glorious inheritance. I also pray that you will understand the incredible greatness of God's power for us who believe Him. This is the same mighty power that raised Christ from the dead and seated Him in the place of honor at God's right hand in the heavenly realms."* Amen!

DAY 3

FACING INJUSTICE

"How can I tolerate your merchants
who use dishonest scales and weights?
The rich among you have become wealthy
through extortion and violence.
Your citizens are so used to lying
that their tongues can no longer tell the truth."
– Micah 6:11-12

In today's society, we hear a lot of debate about truth. Is that true? Or is it fake news or disinformation? Can I trust that or is there a hidden agenda? People adamantly argue for or against all kinds of things, each sure they're right and even vilifying those who disagree with them. It can feel a bit overwhelming if not disheartening, especially when it spills over into churches. Yet, the verses above from Micah 6 remind me this isn't new, unfortunately.

The prophet Micah, whom we're going to look at today, was a contemporary of Hosea and Amos, prophesying during the reigns of Judah's Kings Jotham, Ahaz, and Hezekiah. Based on what we know of ancient history, this was around 750-687 BC when Assyria was the dominant empire.[vii] While we don't know much about him, many decades later, the prophet Jeremiah refers to one of Micah's messages indicating Micah's words made an impact whether or not he saw it in his lifetime.[viii]

We've seen in the last couple days how one of the Israelites' core sins was that they had failed to love God, turning to idolatry. We've also seen their failure to love others. Micah builds on both themes.

Read Micah 6:9-7:6. Jot down the ways God is pointing out their mistreatment of other people.

Does this sound familiar? How do you see injustices like these in our world today?

It can be painful to read, but even more so when we compare that list to injustice that still happens around us. As I'm writing this in the 21st century and see how in some ways, little has changed, it reminds me of these words from King Solomon found in Ecclesiastes 1:9-11, which say,

> *"History merely repeats itself. It has all been done before. Nothing under the sun is truly new. Sometimes people say, "Here is something new!" But actually it is old; nothing is ever truly new. We don't remember what happened in the past, and in future generations, no one will remember what we are doing now."*

Those words were written a couple centuries before Micah's lifetime, but indeed, there is nothing new. People today fail to treat others justly in much the same way as in Micah's day.

Mixed in with the condemnation of the people's behavior were warnings of how God would judge them as a result. While Micah's ministry ended before the people of Judah were exiled, Israel fell to the Assyrians in 722 BC during his lifetime.[ix] He and his contemporaries saw the prophecies against Israel fulfilled before their eyes.

Did you catch the links in Micah 6:16 where he mentions Kings Omri and Ahab? You may remember King Ahab if you're familiar with stories about the prophet Elijah. King Omri was his father and they were two of the most pagan and wicked kings of Israel.[x] Other historical sources indicate Omri was a powerful king who had military successes and brought stability to Israel, but he led the people further away from the LORD.[xi] As for King Ahab, 1 Kings 16:30-33 tells us:

> *"But Ahab son of Omri did what was evil in the LORD's sight, even more than any of the kings before him. And as though it were not enough to follow the example of Jeroboam, he married Jezebel, the daughter of King Ethbaal of the Sidonians, and he began to bow down in worship of Baal. First Ahab built a temple and an altar for Baal in Samaria. Then he set up an Asherah pole. He did more to provoke the anger of the LORD, the God of Israel, than any of the other kings of Israel before him."*

Remember how Yahweh told the Israelites in Exodus 34 not to make treaties with other nations because they would draw them into idol worship? In that same passage, it says that when they made these treaties, they would allow their children to intermarry with these other groups that didn't follow the LORD, which would also lead them into idolatry. Here we see both happening as Ahab made an alliance with Sidon by marrying the Sidonian princess. In the same sentence it also says Ahab brought Baal worship to Israel. Those were dark days for the true worshipers of Yahweh and the people in Micah's day would have known why Micah warned them against following the example set by Omri and Ahab.

But remember the three-part message throughout the prophets? Warning... Judgment... and **Hope**. Despite the people's continual failings and the way they disobeyed God's call to pursue righteousness and justice, He still gave a message of hope through Micah.

> **Read Micah 7:7-20.** Considering how miserably the people had failed to meet God's standards, what jumps out at you in that passage?

I don't know about you, but I find Micah's confidence inspiring. He fully expected God to hear and save him. And then in verse 9, Micah didn't exempt himself from God's judgment. He acknowledged God would punish him for his sin while also trusting God to be just toward him. It can be easy to look at a list of sins and congratulate ourselves on not being like the people who do those things, but even Micah the prophet knew he, too, had sinned.

While I'm skipping ahead chronologically here, it makes me think of this passage from Ezekiel 33:14-16 that says:

> *"And suppose I tell some wicked people that they will surely die, but then they turn from their sins and do what is just and right. For instance, they might give back a debtor's security, return what they have stolen, and obey my life-giving laws, no longer doing what is evil. If they do this, then they will surely live and not die. None of their past sins will be brought up again, for they have done what is just and right, and they will surely live."*

The final part of Micah reminds us that God never changes and keeps His promises. He's the same God who parted the Red Sea and can still work miracles today. In the verses below from Micah 7:18-20, underline the characteristics of God that you see.

> *"Where is another God like You,*
> *who pardons the guilt of the remnant,*
> *overlooking the sins of His special people?*
> *You will not stay angry with Your people forever,*
> *because You delight in showing unfailing love.*

Once again You will have compassion on us.
You will trample our sins under Your feet
and throw them into the depths of the ocean!
You will show us Your faithfulness and unfailing love
as You promised to our ancestors Abraham and Jacob long ago."

Which parts of the passage above do you recognize from Exodus 34:6-7?

Micah points back to when Yahweh made the covenant with Israel and lists characteristics the LORD used to describe Himself in Exodus 34. The people would suffer the consequences of their failure to follow the LORD, but Yahweh's character would stay the same. And even today as we fall short just like the Israelites did, we can still have confidence in the LORD's mercy and love as we seek His forgiveness. Apart from the blood of Jesus, *none* of us are righteous. As it says in Romans 5:6-9,

"When we were utterly helpless, Christ came at just the right time and died for us sinners. Now, most people would not be willing to die for an upright person, though someone might perhaps be willing to die for a person who is especially good. But God showed His great love for us by sending Christ to die for us while we were still sinners. And since we have been made right in God's sight by the blood of Christ, He will certainly save us from God's condemnation."

As you think about the description of God in Micah 7:18-20 and the passage above from Romans 5, what hope or encouragement does it give you today? How have you seen God's love, compassion, and forgiveness in your life in a practical way?

PRAYER FOCUS

As we close today, spend time thanking God for His faithfulness and unfailing love. At the same time, ask God to bring to mind any specific areas where you need to confess ways you've failed to pursue justice for all people, locally and globally. If anything comes to mind, write it down and prayerfully consider any changes you may need to make.

OFFERINGS

"The people of Israel love their rituals of sacrifice,
but to me their sacrifices are all meaningless.
I will hold my people accountable for their sins,
and I will punish them.
They will return to Egypt."
– Hosea 8:13

Both of my parents grew up on farms. By the time I can remember, my dad's parents had moved closer to town, but my maternal grandparents still lived on their land. The dairy cows, sheep and chickens from mom's growing up years were gone, but in their place, grandpa raised goats and grandma had peafowl. Her peacocks often fanned their tail feathers into showy displays as they pranced around and I loved watching them!

In much the same way the male peacocks liked to show off their pretty feathers, though, we people tend to also show off our best sides. On the outside we may look successful and all put together, but be falling apart on the inside.

While we saw yesterday that the people of Israel had turned to idolatry, there were other ways their sin was much more subtle. They went through the motions of doing things God had told them to do, but their hearts were far removed from the LORD. We've already read passages in Hosea, Amos, and Micah and today, we're going back to all three books to look for connections between them.

Read Hosea 8:11-14. What have the people done and what have they not done?

Why are their sacrifices meaningless?

The passage says the people act like they're exempt from Yahweh's laws. The indictment gets even stronger in verse 14 where it says, "Israel has forgotten its Maker." Without saying it outright, we can infer the sacrifices don't mean anything because while the people make outward shows of obedience, they don't actually do what God has asked of them. Just offering sacrifices without obeying the LORD in other areas made the sacrifices worthless. And now, let's compare that to Amos.

Read Amos 5:10-27. What words does Amos use to describe how God sees the people's actions? What will He do with their offerings and praise hymns?

How does this line up with what God told them through the prophet Hosea?

What does God want instead of their offerings and songs?

Again, we see that when people go through the motions of religious rituals, they mean nothing to God if they're done without also following God's other instructions. The people were being hypocrites, acting like they followed the LORD by checking off religious boxes but not actually living out God's teaching daily. We read part of Micah 6 yesterday, but now let's look at the first part of that chapter, too.

Read Micah 6:1-8. Why does Micah bring up Egypt, Moses, Aaron, Miriam, King Balak and Balaam? What should those names have reminded the people about?

Micah reminded them of God's past faithfulness to their people, recalling the pivotal time when God rescued them from Egyptian slavery with Moses, Aaron, and Miriam serving in leadership roles. And while Moabite King Balak wanted Balaam to ask God to curse the Israelites, God told Balaam to bless them instead to Balak's fury.[xii]

How does this passage mirror what Hosea and Amos said?

What do Micah's rhetorical questions tell us about the people's hearts?

While we have less context today for what a temple sacrifice included, Micah's listeners would have known how extravagant an offering "thousands of rams" or "ten thousand rivers of olive oil" would have been. They also knew that while they were to give the firstborn of their flocks and herds, God provided the Passover lamb when Moses led the Israelite slaves out of Egypt in place of requiring them to sacrifice their firstborn sons. Yet, even if they were to go to extremes in what they offered Yahweh, Micah said no, those sacrifices were not what God desired. Instead, in verse eight the LORD asked them "to do what is right, to love mercy, and to walk humbly with your God."

This shouldn't have been a new idea for them. King Solomon summarized this in Proverbs 21:3 and we see a similar idea in one of David's psalms from several hundred years before Micah. As you read, highlight the words and phrases in Psalm 40:6-10 printed below that you saw in the other passages we've read today.

> "You take no delight in sacrifices or offerings.
>   Now that you have made me listen, I finally understand—
>   you don't require burnt offerings or sin offerings.
> Then I said, "Look, I have come.
>   As is written about me in the Scriptures:
> I take joy in doing your will, my God,
>   for your instructions are written on my heart."
> I have told all your people about your justice.
>   I have not been afraid to speak out,
>   as you, O LORD, well know.
> I have not kept the good news of your justice hidden in my heart;
>   I have talked about your faithfulness and saving power.
> I have told everyone in the great assembly
>   of your unfailing love and faithfulness."

Verse 10 has echoes of Exodus 34. David understood what the prophets tried to teach Israel several generations later. He knew what God wanted wasn't the offerings or sacrifices but rather for us to obey God and live justly. Once more, it came down to loving God and loving others. From the Torah to David to the prophets to Jesus—they all point to the same thing.

It's not about the actual sacrifices or offerings—it's about our hearts.

Time and again, the people got it wrong. And let's be honest—many of us get it wrong, too.

We don't offer actual sacrifices on altars now that Jesus paid the price for us by his sacrificial death and resurrection. Yet, we too can fall into the pattern of going to church and checking the religious boxes of our community without living the way God calls us to live. We can be at church on Sunday morning, Sunday night, and Wednesday night; read our Bibles daily; tithe 10% of our income; and even lead a small group Bible study without truly letting our hearts be transformed by God's word.

Where have you noticed yourself checking off religious boxes in your own life? Or are there ways you aren't living in a way that genuinely shows love for God and others?

This can be hard to process, but it's so important to periodically look at our own hearts. If we listen, the Holy Spirit will show us areas where we may have fallen into patterns of just going through the motions or where our hearts aren't in the right place. But just as God still offered hope to the prophets' listeners, we can trust Him to do the same for us.

PRAYER FOCUS

As we close today, spend time in prayer, thanking God for His constant love for us and asking Him to show you where your heart may not be in the right place.
- Are there things you're doing that are *good*, but perhaps with wrong motives?
- Are there any things God may be asking you to do that you haven't done yet?
- What does living justly look like for you?

DAY 5

EVEN SUCH AS THESE

"When we were utterly helpless, Christ came at just the right time and died for us sinners. Now, most people would not be willing to die for an upright person, though someone might perhaps be willing to die for a person who is especially good. But God showed his great love for us by sending Christ to die for us while we were still sinners. And since we have been made right in God's sight by the blood of Christ, he will certainly save us from God's condemnation. For since our friendship with God was restored by the death of his Son while we were still his enemies, we will certainly be saved through the life of his Son. So now we can rejoice in our wonderful new relationship with God because our Lord Jesus Christ has made us friends of God."
– Romans 5:6-11

If you've read many stories from a children's Bible, you may remember one about Jonah and the big fish or whale. I thought it was an amazing story what with Jonah getting swallowed by a big fish and being inside for 3 days! I imagined how smelly that would have been and wondered what it was like in there. If I'm honest, I also judged Jonah since that whole situation happened because he ran away from God. I mean—Jonah was a *prophet* so he knew better, right?!

At the time, I had no idea how many layers were underneath that story. I had no concept for where Nineveh was or why Jonah would have such a dislike for the people who lived there. And I glossed over chapter four if it was even in my children's Bible. To get some context for how this fits with the other prophets we've encountered so far, we're going to read one other passage that mentions this same Jonah.

Read 2 Kings 14:23-27.

King Jeroboam II reigned from 786–746 BC.[xiii] This puts Jonah around the same time both Hosea and Amos began their ministries, and like them, he was a prophet to Israel. There may have also been overlap between Jonah and Micah as well.

Looking at 2 Kings 14:24, what do we learn about Israel's King Jeroboam II? Yet, what do we see God do in 14:27 and why?

While describing Jeroboam II as doing "evil in the LORD's sight," God had Jonah promise Israel military victory through a wicked king. This was not because the king was a good person or obeyed Yahweh, but because God in His mercy chose to save His people from their bitter affliction.

As for Nineveh, today it's located in northern Iraq near Mosul, just east of Syria and just south of Turkey. Back in Jonah's day, it was the capital of Assyria.[xiv] Archaeologists have uncovered writings and pictorial reliefs that record the gruesome ways the Assyrians treated conquered lands.[xv] It's incredibly disturbing to read what they did to people and it's understandable that anyone who heard about these things would have disliked the Assyrians very much.

With that background, **read Jonah 1:1-3.** What do you notice in these verses?

Unlike other prophetic books, this one jumps right into a specific task God gave Jonah and how he purposely did not do it. And because of 2 Kings 14, we already know this isn't the only message God gave Jonah to speak. While the reason isn't immediately clear why he wanted "to get away from the LORD" and avoid speaking God's words to the people of Nineveh, Jonah later tells us the reason in Jonah 4:2, where he says:

> *"Didn't I say before I left home that you would do this, LORD? That is why I ran away to Tarshish! I knew that you are a merciful and compassionate God, slow to get angry and filled with unfailing love. You are eager to turn back from destroying people."*

Where have you seen this description of Yahweh before and why is it significant?

Just like Micah, Jonah describes Yahweh using words straight from Exodus 34. He cites God's character as the reason he didn't want to obey, drawing on the way Yahweh described Himself in Exodus 34:6-7. Jonah didn't want to speak God's message to Nineveh because he knew if they repented, God would relent on punishing them. He had seen God's mercy on Israel despite their king's wickedness and the people's unfaithfulness. And perhaps for the same reason, he felt safe running away from God without expecting dire consequences.

Finish reading Jonah 1. What stands out to you in this chapter?

Did you notice how the sailors took time to ask Jonah questions and try to understand the source of the storm? They could have immediately tried to harm him or get him out of the boat. Instead they asked him questions and tried to return to land rather than throwing him into the sea as he asked.

What do you think would be a characteristic of a successful prophet of the LORD? Is it the same way you would describe a successful missionary? Why or why not?

If a prophet's success is obeying God, then Jonah failed here. Yet, even though Jonah didn't initially go to Nineveh, God still used him to bring repentance to a completely unrelated group of people who didn't know the LORD: the sailors. Jonah wouldn't have met them if he had been obedient to God in the first place. Yet, his testimony to Yahweh's power led them to recognize the one true God. That certainly doesn't mean we should disobey God by flippantly assuming He'll use us anyway, but I do love the reminder that God can redeem our mistakes.

Can you list any examples of when God has used you even when you weren't expecting it or felt unworthy? If so, when?

If you have time, read Jonah 2 which recounts Jonah's prayer while in the fish. In it, we see a glimpse of Jonah's heart toward Yahweh. Then, the story picks back up with Jonah's experience in Nineveh.

Read Jonah 3. How did the Ninevites' response to Jonah's message differ from what we've seen of the Israelites response to Hosea, Amos and Micah?

Here we see the second time when Jonah's words caused heart change, this time across a large city. He may have been reluctant, but once again, God used his message. However, as we keep reading, we'll see how God didn't stop with the Ninevites but kept working on Jonah himself.

Read Jonah 4. How do we see God show mercy, compassion, and love to Jonah?

In what ways have you seen God's mercy, compassion and love toward you even when you didn't deserve it?

While we see some raw emotions from Jonah and an unwilling heart in many ways, I appreciate the honest look at what serving God might feel like.

Thinking about your own life, where do you see yourself in the story?

Do you have anyone or any group of people that you feel reluctant to reach out to, pray for or bless in any way because you don't think they deserve it?

In our polarized society, it can be easy to lump people together and think of them as being one of us or as outsiders. It's also easy to see people like us as the good ones deserving God's favor. We put ourselves on pedestals while giving the "others" less consideration, vilifying them, or even ignoring them.

Thinking back to what Jesus said about the greatest commandments—loving God and our neighbor—all those people who aren't like us still fall into the neighbor category. Jesus himself modeled this over and over, eating with and spending time with people that the "good" religious people looked down on. He also used the story of the Good Samaritan to illustrate this.

Ironically, the people living in Samaria in Jesus' day that the Jewish people hated were descendants of those who lived in Israel in Jonah's day. Just as God sent Jonah to people he thought undeserving, we too may have to wrestle through our own biases (which we may not even know we have) to fulfill the calling God gives us as well.

PRAYER FOCUS

Thinking about where you saw yourself in the story, spend some time reflecting and praying. Is there anything God may be calling you to do? Jot down anything that comes to mind as you spend time talking and listening to the LORD.

<u>Session 2 Group Guide</u>

Before getting together, have everyone complete Session 2.

1.   Open in prayer.

2.   Questions for the group:

- What stood out to you the most about each of these prophets?

    i. Hosea
    ii. Amos
    iii. Micah
    iv. Jonah

- What did you notice about the writing style in each of these books? Did it help to look for passages written in a poetic style?

- Had you thought about how some of the prophets overlapped with each other? Does that impact how you think about them?

- As you read, did you see connections between the different prophets? Or connections to other parts of the Bible?

- Did knowing the three parts to the prophetic message (warning, judgment, hope) impact how you read the passages this week? If so, how?

- Knowing that God called Jonah to speak to Nineveh, what can we see about God's character? How should this impact how Christ followers live today?

- Did any of the reflection questions stand out to you in particular? If so, in what way(s)?

Assyrian Dominance

Session 3
A Moment of Truth

Other Allies

"The people of Israel have become like silly, witless doves,
first calling to Egypt, then flying to Assyria for help.
But as they fly about,
I will throw my net over them
and bring them down like a bird from the sky.
I will punish them for all the evil they do."
– Hosea 7:11-12

I loved history class growing up and read a bunch of biographies as a child. A common theme that seemed to crop up in many of the stories had to do with various wars and conflicts. One country would team up with another to defeat a common enemy who might in turn join forces with even more countries. Despite having different languages and cultures, being united *against* the same thing could become a compelling motivator even if that unity vanished once the shared threat went away.

Back in Exodus when Yahweh made the covenant through Moses, He also warned them against making treaties with outside groups.

Read Exodus 34:12-17. What danger did Yahweh warn would happen if the people made treaties with other peoples?

The LORD knew if the Israelites united themselves with others who did not love Him, they would be drawn away from Him. If we're honest, we've probably all seen that either in our own lives or the lives of people we know. Even if it's not an actual treaty, if we spend a lot of time with people who don't know or follow the LORD, we tend to start behaving more and more like them rather than the other way around.

In the later part of Hosea's ministry, Israel experienced war and internal unrest with several kings and assassinations following Jeroboam II.[i] As they faced threats both internally and externally, the Israelite leaders sought help from other nations rather than relying on Yahweh to protect and guide them.

Read Hosea 7-8. Which parts of the prophetic message do you see in these chapters?
- ☐ Warning of how the people had sinned
- ☐ Pronouncements of judgment for sin
- ☐ Hope of restoration with God

How have they Israelites violated Exodus 34 and what are the consequences?

What imagery does Hosea use to describe the Israelites?

As we also saw in the last session, Hosea accused the people of breaking Yahweh's covenant and promised punishment as a result. Hosea uses a lot of striking poetic descriptions to paint a picture of what will happen. He says God's "fury burns" against them and the idol they made will be "smashed to bits." "They have planted the wind and will harvest the whirlwind." Their crops will wither, there won't be a harvest to eat, and Israel is described as "silly, witless doves," "an old discarded pot," and "a wild donkey looking for a mate".

The military alliances Israel made with other countries revealed a deeper heart issue. Hosea highlighted how the people had "rejected what is good," "appointed kings without [God's] consent, and princes without [God's] knowledge." If you look back at the timeline, you can see how the kings of Israel changed multiple times during Hosea's ministry, sometimes quickly. Hosea 7:7 references this, and 8:14 gets at the reason, saying "Israel has forgotten its Maker and built great palaces." They focused on material things and worldly matters without seeking God first. We'll see a similar indictment against Judah.

Read Isaiah 30:1-17. What sin does Isaiah call out in Judah? What will be the outcome?

Just like Israel, Judah made an alliance with another nation against God's will. The first two verses make it clear the people hadn't sought Yahweh's guidance before seeking foreign help. They also refused to listen to the prophets God sent to point them in the right direction. And despite their attempt to rely on Egypt, they would find themselves disgraced and ashamed.

> **Read Isaiah 30:18-33.** What shift do you see here from the beginning of the chapter? What part of the 3-part prophetic message do you see that wasn't in Hosea 7-8?

While the first 17 verses warned that Judah hadn't followed God and would be punished, verse 18 begins an incredible message of hope. It doesn't negate the first part—the people had still made their own plans and ignored God's direction. But Isaiah tells them it's not too late. If they would seek the LORD and follow His guidance, He would still show them love and compassion because He is a faithful God. (Remember Exodus 34?) Even in their punishment, Yahweh would be with them, teaching them.

> In spite of their failure to rely on God, what does He promise to do? How does Isaiah 30:31-33 contrast with 30:1-7?

Judah sought help from Egypt, but God Himself planned to give them the relief they desired. They went off on their own, trying to make their own solution, but God already had a plan to bring down the Assyrians without an alliance between Judah and Egypt. As I think about how that applies to my own life today, I wonder how often I make decisions without seeking the LORD's direction first or ignoring it when it doesn't match what I want.

Over the years, I can point back to specific times when I asked God about a next step and in my heart, got a very clear answer. Sometimes the answer was a distinct "no" even when I really didn't want it to be. I can't always tell you for sure *why* no was the right answer, although looking back I can see how my life moved in a new direction after some of those turned out to be pivotal decisions.

Another time, I strongly sensed God telling me to "wait" and over the next few weeks, I could see the situation unfolding more clearly and knew God wasn't in it. Rather than just telling me no, however, He guided me to pause and let me see for myself why that was the best answer.

Even when I do seek God's direction, it can sometimes take stepping out one way or another to get a clear answer. As I've done that and continued praying for wisdom, these words from Isaiah 30:21 have often come to mind about how we will hear a voice behind us saying, "This is the way, walk in it, whenever you turn to the right or to the left."[ii] Those words remind me that when I *don't* have clarity, I'm to keep moving forward trusting God to redirect me if I get off course.

Often, God confirms my path by giving me a strong sense of peace or lack thereof. I've had times when I committed to something that seemed good. Later, I've felt a strong sense of uneasiness about the decision that caused me to go back to God in prayer and He made it clear I'd made the wrong choice. More than once, this has led me to reverse a decision I'd made, turning down a job I initially accepted, not moving when I had planned, ending a relationship, and other big decisions. It reminds me of Isaiah 26:3-4, which says,

> *"You will keep in perfect peace*
> *all who trust in you,*
> *all whose thoughts are fixed on you!*
> *Trust in the LORD always,*
> *for the LORD God is the eternal Rock."*

I love how Isaiah describes the peace God gives as "perfect peace", or shalom shalom in Hebrew.[iii] His peace is not dependent on circumstances, but overflows from a heart that focuses on Yahweh, the eternal rock.

As you think about your life today, are there any decisions you need to bring before the LORD to seek His direction? If so, jot them down here and spend some time praying for wisdom and discernment to know His will.

Can you think of times when God has given you a clear answer even if it wasn't the one you wanted to hear? What makes those stand out to you?

Are there any areas of your life where you sense even now that you've gone the wrong direction and feel the Holy Spirit tugging at you to make a change? If so, in what area(s) and what makes you reluctant to listen?

As you reflect on your answers to the last few questions, spend some time in prayer. This might be to thank the LORD for how He's guided you in the past or for how you trust He'll guide you in the future. Or, if you can see areas where you haven't been doing what God's leading you to do, ask Him to show you what your next step needs to be and then follow through. Jot down anything below that comes to mind.

THE WAGES OF SIN

"For the wages of sin is death,
but the free gift of God is eternal life
through Christ Jesus our Lord."
– Roman 6:23

As I write this in late summer looking out over the woods behind my house, I can't help but think of the adage, "you reap what you sow". This year for the first time since I got married, I didn't plant a garden and as a result, we didn't have any fresh produce that I grew myself. I've missed that, but in some ways to be honest, having a break was also nice.

The saying about reaping applies to so many other aspects of life, too. And on the flip side as in my lack of a garden this year, when we don't sow, we won't reap. We can sow seeds that lead to strong friendships, or we can neglect to invest in relationships and find ourselves isolated. We can accomplish all we're asked to do, and more, in a job and hopefully thrive there, or lose said job if we don't meet expectations.

We've seen how Yahweh promised blessing to the Israelites if they obeyed him and on the contrary, warned of punishment for disobedience. To read more examples of this, see Leviticus 26 and Deuteronomy 28 among others. And unfortunately, what we've been reading in the prophets so far has largely given us a case study in what happens when we choose not to obey the LORD. The people of Israel and Judah consistently chose to turn away from Yahweh and eventually reaped the rewards of their disobedience.

Most of the books we've read in so far are fairly short, but several of the prophetic books are much longer. Isaiah is one of the latter and while we read Isaiah 30 yesterday, I want to circle back to get some background on who Isaiah was.

Read Isaiah 1:1 and Isaiah 6. What stands out to you? Remember on the first day of our study how we looked at Ezekiel's call to be a prophet in Ezekiel 2:1-3:14? How was Isaiah's call similar or different?

Isaiah had a vision of Yahweh where He asked, "Whom should I send as a messenger to this people? Who will go for us?" and Isaiah volunteered, saying "Here I am. Send me." And right away, Isaiah received a message to speak to the people that resembles what God told Ezekiel to do. Both were told to take Yahweh's messages to people who wouldn't listen or repent. And while we didn't read Ezekiel 1, his call came out of a vision, too.

While Isaiah lived in Judah and served as a prophet there for the kings who reigned from 792-687 BC, he also prophesied against other nations including Israel. He overlapped with the prophets Hosea, Amos, Jonah and Micah that we've already looked at. During his ministry, Assyria rose to power and a lot happened on the geopolitical scale for both Israel and Judah.

What does the stump imagery in Isaiah 6:13 show?

Because of the people's failure to listen to the prophets and turn back to Yahweh, their land would be devastated like a tree cut down leaving only its stump. Yet, the stump would one day grow again—all hope was not lost.

If you want to read more of the events that happened around the same time for context, see 2 Chronicles 28:1-18. This was when the Syro-Ephraimite War took place. Judah had just experienced crushing defeats at the hands of the armies of Israel and Aram (the Hebrew name for Syria). King Ahaz feared Jerusalem would be captured as well. Isaiah enters the story next.

Read Isaiah 7:1-16. What does Yahweh promise will happen to Israel?

What can you tell about King Ahaz from this passage?

Not only did Isaiah tell Ahaz the attempted invasion of Jerusalem wouldn't happen, but Israel and Aram would themselves be destroyed within 65 years. King Ahaz feared the Israelites and their alliance with Aram, but God remained sovereign and promised to protect Judah.

It's interesting to me that God sent Isaiah to King Ahaz with this encouraging prophecy even though the king had not sought God's help. Remember how in Jonah's time God used evil King Jeroboam II to bring relief to Israel because of His love for His people? God's salvation for Judah during King Ahaz's reign reminds me of that where yet again we see God grant relief to His people in spite of a wicked ruler. Ahaz even refused to cooperate when Isaiah told him to ask for a sign to confirm the prophecy would be true, causing Isaiah to ask how long Ahaz would exhaust Yahweh's patience.

2 Kings 16:5 tells us the prophecy came true:

> *"Then King Rezin of Aram and King Pekah of Israel came up to attack Jerusalem. They besieged Ahaz but could not conquer him."*

Unfortunately, Ahaz didn't turn to the LORD even after God saved them from their enemies and the end of Isaiah 7 warns of future danger from Assyria. This warning came true during the reign of Ahaz as recorded in 2 Chronicles 28:16-25.

If Ahaz recognized God's role in protecting Jerusalem from capture by Israel and Aram, we don't see evidence of it. So, Yahweh allowed Edom and the Philistines to invade Judah. Ahaz turned to the king of Assyria for help, but the Assyrians attacked Judah instead. As a result, Ahaz gave them valuable items from the temple as tribute. Even worse, he worshiped the gods of Aram, thinking they were more powerful than Yahweh, and closed the temple of the LORD.

> Think of times when you've seen God provide for you, your family, or friends. How have you responded? Has His provision caused you to change how you live and reorient yourself to following Him?

We have one more passage to read today that shows the fulfillment of an ongoing prophecy we've seen spoken through each of Yahweh's prophets to Israel.

Read 2 Kings 17:1-23.

This passage provides the historical record of how God punished Israel just as He promised. Over and over, He sent prophets with warnings to repent, but the

Israelites refused. And then just as God said He would, and shortly after King Ahaz' death, the nation of Israel was destroyed just as the prophets foretold.

> What resonates with you the most from what we've read today? In what ways can you apply this to your own life?

I imagine we may each have different answers to that question. For me personally, I find hope in knowing God still loved Israel even when they reached rock bottom. His offer of restoration never goes away even when He lets us experience the consequences for our sins. With His help, we can find freedom from sin patterns that may feel impossible to break. He never changes and with His help, our fickle hearts can.

The passages we've read also remind me our God keeps His promises. We can claim them as truth even when we can't see how He'll fulfill them.

> Can you think of any promises that God has given you, either directly in some way or as you've studied His word? How have you seen those fulfilled? Or, are you still waiting?

Prayer Focus

Spend time praying, thanking God for ways He offers you hope today. At the same time, are there any areas you sense the Holy Spirit prompting you to confess? Or, do you have a heavy heart about areas of your life where you're losing hope? Ask the LORD if He has anything to say about those situations and if He brings anything to mind, trust He will do what He says even it seems surprising.

God's Instrument

"What sorrow awaits Assyria, the rod of my anger.
I use it as a club to express my anger.
I am sending Assyria against a godless nation,
against a people with whom I am angry.
Assyria will plunder them,
trampling them like dirt beneath its feet.
But the king of Assyria will not understand that he is my tool;
his mind does not work that way.
His plan is simply to destroy,
to cut down nation after nation."
– Isaiah 10:5-7

Some things may always be a mystery. Just because we think we understand something on a logical level doesn't mean it always makes sense. Enter the Assyrian Empire. Remember when we read in Jonah and talked about how evil the Assyrians were to other people? Yet, despite how awful the Assyrians were, God used them as part of His larger plan to judge Israel.

Isaiah gives us insight into this as we just read in the verses above. We're going to pick back up in that passage.

Read Isaiah 10:7-11. Looking at the whole passage (v. 5-11), what stands out to you?

Seeing that God not only allowed Assyria to conquer Israel, but actually *sent* Assyria against His people makes me pause. This wasn't random coincidence, but rather divine orchestration.

Why did Yahweh do this and how may it relate to events today?

God gave warnings through the prophets over and over for centuries, but Israel as a whole refused to listen and repent. And so, as punishment, God Himself raised up an enemy to bring calamity on the people He loved. In this case, that enemy was wicked Assyria.

> Look back at Isaiah 10:5-7 printed at the beginning of today's lesson. What word or synonyms do you see repeated several times?

The New Living Translation refers to God's anger and says He was angry. The original Hebrew uses three different words though: *appi* (of My anger), *zami* (My indignation), and *ebrati* (of My wrath).[iv] Anger is a word I would use, but indignation and wrath seem much stronger somehow. The word indignation makes me think of a more righteous anger, which fits with the description of Israel being a godless nation. They had earned God's wrath, provoking Him with their profane, hypocritical behavior.

The rest of the passage we just read focuses on Assyria and how in spite of God using it to accomplish His purpose, the king of Assyria didn't recognize Yahweh's role in his success. Isaiah refers to Assyria as a rod, a club, and God's tool. There was more going on than was immediately obvious.

> **Read Isaiah 10:12-19**. How does this passage build on the last part of what we read in verses 5-11 to paint a picture of the Assyrian king? What fatal flaw is God pointing out in the king and what does He promise will be the result?

> How does verse 15 play on verses 5 and 7?

> What analogy does Isaiah use in verses 16-19 to represent God and Assyria?

God used a nation that history shows us used brutal, evil military tactics to punish His people. But because that nation, too, particularly its king, did not acknowledge the LORD's involvement, they too would fall to another nation.[v]

The prophet Nahum also prophesied against Assyria. We know little about him except that he was from Elkosh. We don't know for sure when he lived, but Nahum 3:8-10 refers to the fall of Egypt's capital city, Thebes, as a past event, which happened in 663 BC. He also refers to the future fall of Nineveh, which happened in 612 BC, so Nahum prophesied sometime between the demise of those two cities.[vi]

Read Nahum 1. What similarity do you see between Nahum and Isaiah 10:5-19?

Just as in the Isaiah passage, we see again here that God is angry with Assyria and will punish it for its evil ways. Even though it looked like the ungodly were literally getting away with murder, the LORD saw and knew their evil. God used them to punish His unfaithful people, but He didn't make them evil, and Assyria deserved punishment for its own wickedness, too. We see the same imagery of the LORD as a fire in Nahum just like in Isaiah.

Thinking back to what we read in the book of Jonah, what contrast do you see between the people of Nineveh in Jonah's day compared to Nahum's time?

What similarity do you see between Nahum 1:2 and Exodus 34:14?

> "You must worship no other gods, for the LORD, whose very name is Jealous, is a God who is jealous about His relationship with you."
> –*Exodus 34:14*

Here we see Yahweh is jealous for His name. The people turned to other places for fulfillment, but God wanted an exclusive relationship with them.

What similarity do you see in Nahum 1:3, Exodus 34:6, and Jonah 4:2?

> "The LORD passed in front of Moses, calling out, "Yahweh! The LORD! The God of compassion and mercy! I am slow to anger and filled with unfailing love and faithfulness."
> –*Exodus 34:6*

> "So he complained to the LORD about it: "Didn't I say before I left home that you would do this, LORD? That is why I ran away to Tarshish! I knew that you are a merciful and compassionate God, slow to get angry and filled with unfailing love. You are eager to turn back from destroying people."
> –*Jonah 4:2*

Jonah showed us that God was willing to forgive the Assyrians for their sins and did exactly that when they repented. However, by Nahum's time maybe 100 years later, the people had returned to their wicked ways. Their repentance was short-lived and so too then was their reprieve from God's punishment.

Sin requires a penalty no matter who we are or where we're from. If the Assyrian king had recognized God's sovereignty rather than being proud and arrogant, he would have had a different outcome even though he wasn't from God's chosen people. And the Israelites themselves *were* God's chosen people, but He brought the consequences for their sins squarely upon them.

Read Isaiah 10:20-34. Looking back at what we read before, what irony do you see between verses 15 and 34?

Are there any things happening in our world today that make you question why God doesn't intervene to cause a different outcome? If so, what/where?

Again, we see God's promise that Assyria would fall. An ax would come against them just as they were like an ax to Israel. While we may not recognize His hand at work, God is sovereign over all geopolitical events. As I type these words, I could point to conflicts and rumors of war around the world that cause alarm for many. Yet, seeing how God was at work back in Isaiah and Nahum's lifetimes reminds me He's still on the throne now.

What we've read today also reminds us of *who* God is. Because of His unchanging nature, Isaiah confidently pointed toward a time when a remnant would return to their land. God didn't plan to destroy them completely and this remnant would depend on Yahweh, trusting Him rather than alliances. Yet, because the LORD is jealous for His relationship with His people, He rooted out wickedness even when it meant punishing those He loved.

PRAYER FOCUS

As we close today, spend time quietly before the LORD. Jot down anything that comes to mind and pray as you feel the Holy Spirit leading you, whether in thanksgiving, confession, or anything else on your heart or mind.

Even Judah

"Learn to do good.
Seek justice.
Help the oppressed.
Defend the cause of orphans.
Fight for the rights of widows."
– Isaiah 1:17

They say those who don't know history are doomed to repeat it. I've been thinking about that a lot lately, both in terms of current world events and in looking at cultural trends in my own country. It may be more noticeable on a smaller level where we see predictable consequences in people's lives for the choices they make. Yet, we can also see it on a collective society level, too. We may feel powerless to impact the larger trends as we see them unfold, but we may find we can do more than we thought if we take a closer look at *what* allowed the situation in the first place.

I wonder if that's a little how it was for Judah. We saw earlier that some of the prophets who spoke against Israel pointed out Judah's faithfulness to God. And yet, the people of Judah ultimately slipped into the same behavior as Israel. Prophets tried to point them back to the right way, but the decline continued.

> **Read Isaiah 1:1-20.** What similarities do you see between what Isaiah calls out in the people of Judah and what the prophets we've already read pointed out in the people of Israel?

Isaiah declared that the people of Judah had rebelled against God, failing to recognize His care for them. God rejected their offerings because of their hypocrisy, their festivals and celebrations for being sinful and false, and their prayers because of their injustice toward others. They went through the motions of obedience, but God saw through to their hearts. Sound familiar? We saw these exact things called out against the Israelites.

And did you notice the past reference he included in verses 9-10? Once again, we see a comparison to Sodom and Gomorrah. Between that and when Isaiah described the country lying in ruins with Jerusalem abandoned, it should have set off alarm bells in the people's minds. Just as God had brought disaster on Israel for their sins, He was about to do the same to Judah.

But just as Isaiah and the other prophets promised God would be merciful to the people of Israel and Judah if they turned back to God, He offers the same hope to us today. In verses 16-17, Isaiah lists very tangible ways the people could demonstrate heart change:

> *"Learn to do good. Seek justice. Help the oppressed. Defend the cause of orphans. Fight for the rights of widows."*

And if that sounds familiar, it parallels what we read in Micah 6:8:

> *"No, O people, the LORD has told you what is good, and this is what He requires of you: to do what is right, to love mercy, and to walk humbly with your God."*

At the same time, it's clear that just doing the right things with the wrong heart wasn't what God wanted either. The way they treated God and others served as a barometer for what they had on the inside.

> How does the poetic imagery in Isaiah 1:18-20 tie to Jesus?

In a similar way, the blood of Jesus takes away the stain of our sins. God looks at our hearts and sees whether we're repentant and seeking Him. He is all the things He calls us to be as well, but He also understands our failings. As it says in Hebrews 4:14-16,

> *"So then, since we have a great High Priest who has entered heaven, Jesus the Son of God, let us hold firmly to what we believe. This High Priest of ours understands our weaknesses, for He faced all of the same testings we do, yet He did not sin. So let us come boldly to the throne of our gracious God. There we will receive His mercy, and we will find grace to help us when we need it most."*

We need someone to save us just like the people of Judah.

Read Isaiah 1:21-31. In verses 21-22, what echoes do you see of what Judah had been like in the past?

Isaiah reminded the people they were once faithful and like pure silver. He describes Judah in the past as the "home of justice and righteousness." He contrasts these images by describing Judah in his day as a prostitute (not faithful), filled with murderers (no longer just and righteous), and worthless slag (no longer pure silver).

If you compare your past walk with God to now, how does it compare? Are you growing in your relationship with the LORD?

It's easy to read those strong words and gloss over how they apply to our own lives, but at some point we all have had times when we too weren't completely faithful to God's ways, were unjust, unrighteous, or in need of refining. And if you read that with a heavy heart thinking, I have all of those failings, you're in good company. As we've talked about before, none of us are righteous, none worthy of God's forgiveness on our own merits.

As with other passages we've read, Isaiah 1 ends with a call to obedience while guaranteeing punishment if the people of Judah refused to turn back to God. There's something so powerful in the last line that says, "I, the LORD, have spoken!" While Isaiah was the messenger, he reminded them that the words he was telling them had come from Yahweh Himself.

Remember King Ahaz that we read about yesterday? His son, Hezekiah, became the next king after him. King Hezekiah was the last king listed during Isaiah's ministry and Isaiah 36-39 tells the story of how he sought God's help when Assyria attacked Judah again. He responded very differently than his father.

Read Isaiah 37. How does God respond to Hezekiah?

How does Isaiah's prophecy illustrate what could have happened for Israel if they had heeded the prophets' warnings?

This is such a breath of fresh air after all the warnings of judgment that came true. Because Hezekiah truly sought Yahweh and put his trust in Him, God protected Jerusalem and did not allow Assyria to conquer the land. Judah had strayed from the LORD as we saw in Isaiah 1, but here we see how God kept His promise to show favor to those who called on His name.

If you keep reading in Isaiah 38-39, you'll see that Isaiah warned King Hezekiah that Jerusalem would fall to Babylon. While Hezekiah's humility before the LORD resulted in a reprieve from the coming judgment, God knew it wouldn't last. King Hezekiah's son, Manasseh, became one of the most evil kings Judah had seen as you can read in 2 Kings 20:21-21:1-16. Second Chronicles 33:22-23 tells us Manasseh's son who reigned next was just as evil.

While we can hope our example points others to follow the LORD, even kings can only control so much. We have no guarantees about what the future will hold with so much uncertainty in our world. Yet, we can still trust that our God is the same one who reigned during Hezekiah's day.

PRAYER FOCUS

As we close today ask the LORD to show you anything you need to see. If it helps, jot down things as they come to mind.
- What do you have to be thankful for?
- Are there any areas that He brings to mind that you need to confess and turn from?
- Have you believed any lies about His character and His ability to forgive anything you've done?

DAY 5

AN UNDOING

"What sorrow awaits rebellious, polluted Jerusalem,
the city of violence and crime! ...
But the LORD is still there in the city,
and He does no wrong.
Day by day He hands down justice,
and He does not fail.
But the wicked know no shame."
– Zephaniah 3:1, 5

Have you ever worked hard to make something happen only to later see it come apart? It's disheartening to say the least. It's especially painful when the hard work was to guide someone, a child perhaps, on the right path only to watch in despair when a completely different direction gets chosen. Unfortunately, what we've studied so far has shown us this dynamic at work between our Heavenly Father and the people of the prophets' time. Today, we'll see that again.

As we read in the book of Zephaniah, we're still in the time when the Assyrian empire was dominant. It had been nearly 80 years since Assyria wiped out the nation of Israel in 722 BC. Like Isaiah, Zephaniah lived in Judah, but Manasseh and Amon had come and gone, leaving Amon's young son, Josiah, as the new king. During his reign from 640-609 BC, Assyrian power declined leading up to Nineveh's fall to Babylon in 612 BC.[vii]

Zooming in a bit, we're going to take a closer look at a couple significant things that happened while Josiah was king. Second Chronicles 34 tells us in verses 2-3 and 8:

"He [Josiah] did what was pleasing in the LORD's sight and followed the example of his ancestor David. He did not turn away from doing what was right. During the eighth year of his reign, while he was still young, Josiah began to seek the God of his ancestor David. Then in the twelfth year he began to purify Judah and Jerusalem, destroying all the pagan shrines, the Asherah poles, and the carved idols and cast images. ... In the eighteenth year of his reign, after he had purified the land and the Temple, Josiah appointed Shaphan son of Azaliah, Maaseiah the governor of Jerusalem, and Joah son of Joahaz, the royal historian, to repair the Temple of the LORD his God."

During this time of repairing the temple, verse 14b tells us "Hilkiah the priest found the Book of the Law of the LORD that was written by Moses." Did you catch the action verb there? Hilkiah **found** the book of the law. As in, the priests apparently did not know where it was and quite possibly had never seen it. Rabbinical tradition says it had been hidden in the Temple treasury to keep King Ahaz, Hezekiah's father, from burning it.[viii] If not Ahaz, it certainly seems plausible it might have needed hidden during Manasseh's reign as well. Keep this background in mind as we continue.

Read Zephaniah 1. What stands out to you about Zephaniah's family background as listed in verse 1?

Unlike other prophets, did you notice that his genealogy goes back to his great, great grandfather, Hezekiah? If this refers to King Hezekiah, the current King Josiah's great grandfather, then Zephaniah and Josiah could have been distant cousins.[ix] His dad's name also had a tie to another power of that day, Cush.

What sins does Zephaniah accuse the priests and people of Judah of committing?

The sins Zephaniah calls out sound like the same ones other prophets mentioned. Remember how we've seen how biblical authors use their word choice to link to other parts of the Bible? Here, Zephaniah uses figurative language to link back to the first part of Genesis.

Read Genesis 1:20-31 and Genesis 2:7.

In Zephaniah 1:2-3, we see the undoing of this part of the Genesis creation story:

"'I will sweep away everything
   from the face of the earth,' says the LORD.
'I will sweep away people and animals alike.   [undoing of creation story day 6]
   I will sweep away the birds of the sky and   [undoing of creation story day 5]
   the fish in the sea.
I will reduce the wicked to heaps of rubble,   [wordplay in Hebrew: adam is the
   and I will wipe humanity from the face of   Hebrew word for mankind and adamah
   the earth,' says the LORD."   is the Hebrew word for dirt, earth, or
                                                ground—the very thing Adam was
                                                created from in Genesis 2:7[x]]

77

Let's also compare that to Genesis 6:5-7 below on why God sent the flood during Noah's time:

> "The LORD observed the extent of human wickedness on the earth, and He saw that everything they thought or imagined was consistently and totally evil. So the LORD was sorry He had ever made them and put them on the earth. It broke His heart. And the LORD said, "I will wipe this human race I have created from the face of the earth. Yes, and I will destroy every living thing—all the people, the large animals, the small animals that scurry along the ground, and even the birds of the sky. I am sorry I ever made them."

Zephaniah's listeners should have seen a parallel between the punishment Zephaniah pronounced against them and the judgment sent back in the time of Noah.

Because Josiah tried to bring reforms to point people back to God, Zephaniah, like Isaiah, saw some progress at the leadership level. Because King Josiah humbled his heart before the LORD, God promised in 2 Chronicles 34:26-28 that Judah's punishment for breaking the covenant with Yahweh would not happen until after Josiah's lifetime. But this also showed that Judah would still be punished for not following the LORD. While the punishment would be delayed, it was coming.

Read Zephaniah 3:1-8. How do these prophecies relate to what we've already read today?

Again, we see a promise that God would punish Judah for its sins. If the people knew the book of the law had been found and that God's judgment was coming for their sins, this message should have been very sobering. If they knew the reason Israel had fallen to Assyria—for not following the LORD—this should have caused even more concern and heart repentance. Yet, we also see a message of future hope in Zephaniah.

Read Zephaniah 3:9-20. What stands out to you in this passage?

Here again we see the third part of the prophetic message, hope! Did you notice anything interesting about verses 9-10? Just as Zephaniah 1:2-3 had an undoing of the Genesis creation story which goes badly for the world, here we see the undoing of the Genesis 11:5-7 account of the Tower of Babel, printed below.[xi]

> *"But the LORD came down to look at the city and the tower the people were building. 'Look!' He said. 'The people are united, and they all speak the same language. After this, nothing they set out to do will be impossible for them! Come, let's go down and confuse the people with different languages. Then they won't be able to understand each other.'"*

The Hebrew word for language in Genesis 11 is the same one used in Zephaniah 3.[xii] Unlike the harmful undoing of God's creation in Zephaniah 1, here we see the purification of the people's language (lips) where they had been confused in Genesis 11.[xiii] What's more, Zephaniah 3 goes on to show the restoration he's prophesying would be for more than just the people of Judah. By saying it extended "beyond the rivers of Cush" (Ethiopia), he's using an inclusive picture where the scattering that happened at the Tower of Babel will be undone across the nations.[xiv]

Where do you want to see restoration in our world or in your personal life? What hope does this undoing and restoration language offer for us today?

PRAYER FOCUS

Are there areas of your life where you long to see something undone or restored? Where do you need the LORD to work a miracle? Spend time lifting those cares and concerns to God. Ask if He has anything to show you about them and jot down anything that comes to mind.

Going Deeper

Second Kings 21:2 tells us King Manasseh "did what was evil in the LORD's sight," and gives a summary of the idolatry he not only followed but led the people of Judah into as well. God sent prophets to condemn Manasseh's behavior and warn that as a result of the sins he led Judah to commit, Jerusalem would be destroyed just like Samaria. Manasseh did not heed their warnings.

While Nahum's ministry lines up with the time when Manasseh reigned, it's interesting to me that Nahum's recorded prophecy was against Assyria and none of the other prophetic books come from this time period. As I researched that, the commentaries I read said the innocent blood Manasseh shed in 2 Kings 21:16 included the murder of prophets and was alluded to in Jeremiah 2:30.[xv] Sadly, tradition indicates even the prophet Isaiah may have been one of these martyred.[xvi] Manasseh's lengthy reign was a dark time for those who were faithful to the LORD.

While we may not personally find ourselves in physical danger for following God, we can likely think of areas where Christians are persecuted on many levels. But even then, all hope is not lost, and Manasseh's story illustrates that. Showing how God meant it when He promised hope for those who repent, 2 Chronicles 33:10-18 includes an account of how God got through to Manasseh while he was a prisoner in Assyria. Because he repented, the LORD brought him back to Jerusalem.

It's unclear how much longer Manasseh ruled after this heart change. Second Chronicles 33:22-23 tells us his son, Amon, followed in his father's original wicked footsteps during his short two years as king.

Just having a leader or parent who tries to follow Yahweh is not enough. We see that in the progression of these four kings: Ahaz (wicked), his son Hezekiah (good), his son Manasseh (very wicked until later in life repentance), and then his son Amon (wicked). We're still accountable for our own choices. When we repent of our sins and seek the LORD wholeheartedly, we may see a powerful impact from that in our own sphere of influence. Yet, even if we don't see that impact, we can trust that as we seek God, He'll use us for His glory even when we can't see how.

Before getting together, have everyone complete Session 3.

1. Open in prayer.

2. Questions for the group:

    - In what area(s) do you find yourself relying on God most? Or in what area(s) do you struggle to rely on Him first or have a hard time trusting Him? Why?

    - Have you had a time when God clearly gave you direction? How did you know?

    - What surprising things have you seen God use in your life?

    - Thinking about our world today, are there any things God may be moving, shaking, or making happen whether it's what you'd have chosen? How do you think God might use those things?

    - In what area(s) do you tend to compare yourself to others and feel relieved because you're not as bad as them? Where might God still want you to do more toward loving God and others?

    - How could God use your story or influence to draw others to the LORD?

Babylonian Dominance

SESSION 4
JUDGMENT AND HOPE

DAY 1

FOR A PURPOSE

"I have told you these things before they happen so that when they do happen, you will believe."
– John 14:29

I wouldn't put suffering at the top of a list of things I'd like to do. But if I'm going to go through hardship, I at least want to know *why*. And so often, the reason for difficult things may not be readily apparent. Or *ever* apparent. It's hard to reconcile God being sovereign with the tragic things that may happen in our lives, the lives of people we love, or simply what we see from a distance. If God could have stopped it, why didn't He?

Today we'll see Habakkuk had questions for God about what was going on in his country. The book doesn't give us any specific dates, but it appears to have been before one of the times Babylon invaded Judah. Based on that limited info, his prophecies may have been written around 586 BC, 597 BC, or possibly as late as 605 BC.[i] This puts his ministry at least 80 years after prophets like Isaiah and Hosea.

On a geopolitical level, Israel fell to Assyria in 722 BC, Assyria's capital Nineveh was defeated by Babylon in 612 BC, and Assyria allied itself to Egypt. The next few years saw Judah caught between the Egyptians to the south and Babylon to the northeast. Judah's kings switched alliances between the two depending on who looked to be stronger until 597 BC when Judah's new young King Jehoichin surrendered to Babylon. They exiled him and other leading members of Judah to Babylon, including the prophet Ezekiel, leaving the king's uncle as a new puppet ruler until 586 BC.[ii] Somewhere in the turmoil of those times, God spoke to the prophet Habakkuk.

Read Habakkuk 1-2. As you read, complete the table which continues on the next page.

	Who is speaking?	What does the speaker want?
Habakkuk 1:1-4		

	Who is speaking?	How does this answer the previous passage?
Habakkuk 1:5-11		
Habakkuk 1:12-2:1		
Habakkuk 2:2-20		

Habakkuk clearly felt troubled by what he saw going on in Judah. He questioned why God didn't seem to be listening or doing anything (1:1-4). God responded that He was bringing the Babylonians to judge Judah (1:5-11). Habakkuk then asked why God who is "pure and cannot stand the sight of evil" would allow evil people to succeed at the expense of more righteous ones (1:12-2:1). God assured Habakkuk the evil would certainly be judged at the hands of the Babylonians, but also promised Babylon would be judged, too (2:2-20).

This reminds me of what we saw with Nahum's prophecies about Assyria. God used Assyria to judge Israel, but Assyria's atrocities brought judgment on itself as well. Here we see the same dynamic with Judah and Babylon. God's plans aren't in a vacuum and while it may seem like evil wins for a season, God has an appointed time when He will set His plans in motion. I find Habakkuk 2:2-3 particularly moving:

> "Then the LORD said to me,
> 'Write my answer plainly on tablets,
>   so that a runner can carry the correct message to others.
> This vision is for a future time.
>   It describes the end, and it will be fulfilled.
> If it seems slow in coming, wait patiently,
>   for it will surely take place.
>   It will not be delayed.'"

This mirrors what Jesus told His disciples in John 14:29 where He told them what was going to happen in advance so when it happened, they would know it was done by the LORD. Similarly, Yahweh told Habakkuk to write down what God told him would happen and assured him it would certainly happen even if it seemed delayed.

That reminds me of something that happened to Daniel as well. He was one of those exiled to Babylon and we'll look at his story more later, too.

> For now, **read Daniel 10:11-14**. What stands out to you the most in this passage?

> What encouragement can you find in it for yourself today?

This passage often makes me cry. I find it so moving that God sent Daniel a clear reassurance that his prayers had been heard even though he wouldn't see the answer fulfilled yet. In this case, he waited 21 days, but many times I've waited years before I've seen the answers I've prayed for or understood what God meant when He showed me something in advance.
Waiting is so hard, especially when like Habakkuk those seasons leave me wondering if I misheard God or why there's a delay. Experience has taught me to keep pressing in, trusting, and waiting for God will certainly fulfill all His plans. And out of those seasons of waiting, He has brought tremendous growth in my faith.

Did God ultimately bring the judgment Habakkuk expected? Yes, but not how he thought. Like Jonah who wanted God to judge the Ninevites for their evil ways, Habakkuk was also waiting to see God judge his people for their wickedness. He didn't expect or want it to be at the hands of the Babylonians, though.

Warning and judgment—parts one and two of the typical prophetic message. But the final chapter of Habakkuk brings us to the third part of the message as well—**hope**.

Read Habakkuk 3, and as you read, look for how he describes Yahweh. How does Habakkuk describe God in this passage?

In verses 17-19, where has Habakkuk placed his hope?

I love how Habakkuk made it clear he knew God's character and power. He trusted Yahweh would judge evil and save His people. But I find his closing lines even more powerful as he said that even if God *didn't* do what he knew God *could* do, he would still rejoice in the LORD who gave him strength. He knew God was his provider even if what God provided didn't look like he expected.

Even if the fig trees, fruit vines, olive trees, and fields didn't produce anything—even if the sheep and cows vanished—even then Habakkuk restated his trust in Yahweh. This certainly isn't a prosperity gospel type of hope built on material things, but a bedrock trust in the LORD's character. Habakkuk knew God was sovereign and committed to "rejoice in the LORD" and "be joyful in the God of [his] salvation" even if current circumstances didn't look good. As God brought judgment on Judah, he knew things would look bleak for a time, perhaps the rest of his own lifetime, but his faith in the LORD was unshaken.

This proclamation of hope differs from the promises of future restoration we've seen from some of the other prophets. Yet, I love how Habakkuk reminds us to look beyond what we may see with our physical eyes. Just as Daniel had to wait even for a short time to see God's answer, Habakkuk believed God's promise to fulfill His word in His time, however long it took.

And so, my questions to myself, and to you, are:

Where have you seen this in your own life in the past? Where have you waited on God and seen Him fulfill His word, even if it took a while?

Where are you currently waiting on the LORD?

It can be so hard to be in a time of waiting and wondering when God will respond, when He will act. If you're in a season of waiting, don't be discouraged or give up hope in the God of our salvation. Though this time may last far longer than you ever dreamed, we have a faithful God who keeps His promises even if you don't see the fruit you hoped for or the physical circumstances you expected.

PRAYER FOCUS

As we close today, spend time in prayer, thanking God for how you've seen Him move in your life and for any promises He has given you—confessing times when your faith has become weak—renewing your commitment to wait on Him—asking Him to intervene in areas you haven't yet released to Him. Whatever your circumstances and no matter where you may be on the waiting spectrum, rest assured that He hears your prayers and loves you very much.

DAY 2

BROKEN CISTERNS

"For my people have done two evil things:
They have abandoned me—
the fountain of living water.
And they have dug for themselves cracked cisterns
that can hold no water at all!"
– Jeremiah 2:13

It's funny how our minds make associations between things, often unconsciously. As if on cue, just thinking about mental associations reminds me of a story about Pavlov's dogs correlating a bell with food that I heard in a psych class years ago. I guess my professor should be glad it stuck! And I can hear a song from the past and immediately have certain feelings and memories pop up.

I have something similar with Jeremiah 2:13. In the summer of 2007, God led me on a journey into the proverbial wilderness moving from the Midwest to Colorado. It was the start of a season where my faith grew exponentially. Not long after my move, I vividly remember my new pastor reading from Jeremiah 2 and was struck by verse 13 in particular. The version he read from referred to the people digging "broken cisterns" and as I was sorting through my own faith, it really resonated with me.

We've seen how prophets pointed out the people's tendency to replace God with other things in their lives, and this metaphor of a cracked, broken cistern made that seem more tangible to me. And I guess that was Jeremiah's intent in the first place— to use poetic imagery to illustrate how the people's attempts to follow their own way had failed.

Before we look more at Jeremiah 2, though, let's back up and get an idea of who Jeremiah was and where he fits in the big picture of Israel and Judah.

Read Jeremiah 1:1-3. Can you tell where Jeremiah ties into what we've looked at so far?

Remember when we read about King Josiah in the last session? Because Jeremiah's call happened in Josiah's thirteenth year, we can tell from 2 Chronicles 34 that this was five years after Josiah began his religious reforms and five years before Hilkiah the priest, likely Jeremiah's father, found the book of the law. Young Jeremiah would have seen spiritual reformation firsthand.

But in 2 Chronicles 34:22-28 the prophet Huldah warned Josiah that after his death God would bring the judgment warned about in the book of the law. Thirteen years after that warning, for reasons that aren't immediately clear, Josiah put himself in the wrong place to fight a battle God hadn't called him to fight.

Read 2 Chronicles 35:20-25.

This story always makes me sad. It serves as another reminder that even those of us who try to follow the LORD must still be careful to seek His direction. Who knows what might have happened had Josiah heeded Neco's warning, but since he didn't, it led to his death and started the final chain of events leading up to Jerusalem's fall.

What can you tell about Jeremiah's status at the time of Josiah's death?

Jeremiah must have had a prominent role during Josiah's lifetime since he was the one to compose funeral songs for the fallen king. While they aren't in Jeremiah's book of lamentations found in our Bible, he seems to have been a gifted songwriter.

Read Jeremiah 1:4-19. What did God call Jeremiah to do and what did Yahweh promise him?

God called Jeremiah to be a prophet to nations, not just to Judah. The Babylonians knew of him and showed him favor when they destroyed Jerusalem.[iii] And as far as we know, he spent his final time on earth living in Egypt albeit against his wishes.[iv] Whether he saw people from other nations draw near to the LORD or not, God made it clear in the beginning that He had called Jeremiah to speak to more than just Judah.

Jeremiah has been called the Weeping Prophet because of his poems and songs expressing deep sorrow over his people's ongoing failure to repent. While many other prophets spoke about future destruction, Jeremiah lived long enough to see God's judgment on Judah firsthand. Between persecution, a drawn-out enemy siege and ultimately dying in a foreign land, he went through a lot of really hard things. However, history vindicated his prophecies despite the persecution he experienced in his lifetime.

Now that we have some background on Jeremiah, let's circle back to chapter 2 and those broken cisterns.

> **Read Jeremiah 2:1-13.** What imagery does Jeremiah use as a comparison for Jerusalem (Judah) and its past relationship with the LORD? Where have we seen this before?

> What ultimate charge is the LORD making against Judah and how does it relate to the cistern analogy in verse 13?

The first part of this chapter makes me think of Hosea's prophecies to Israel because it compares Jerusalem to a young bride. In the past the people of Judah were eager to please the LORD, but that had changed over the years. God asked them through Jeremiah what He had done to cause them to turn away from Him and worship idols. To simplify the charges, He lumped the people's sins into two groups: abandoning God, "the fountain of living water," and instead, digging their own cisterns that cannot hold water.

> In what ways have you tried to meet your own needs on your own rather than seeking God?

No matter how alienated we may feel from God's hope, He offers salvation to each of us. In the offer of living water, though, we have a choice just like the people of Jeremiah's day. To accept the living water means following the LORD. To reject the living water means choosing our own way, seeking after our own broken cisterns to satisfy us.

Read Jeremiah 3:11-4:2. Which parts of the 3-part prophetic message do you see (warning, judgment, hope)?

How does Yahweh describe Himself in verse 12 and what does the passage say He longs for?

Jeremiah 3:12 echoes part of Exodus 34:6 where God says He's merciful. Again, despite how the people broke God's covenant and earned punishment for refusing to repent, God still offered hope of restoration. This is the same basic message we see over and over in the books of the prophets.

In what areas do you struggle to believe and accept God's hope? What makes it difficult?

PRAYER FOCUS

As we close, spend time reflecting on the hope God offers. How have you responded? Are there ways you need to repent, perhaps for not believing God's truths or for keeping them from others? Have you believed any lies about God's character and His love and mercy for you? Ask the LORD to reveal to you whether there's any action you need to take and thanking Him for including us in His offer of salvation.

DAY 3

DECEITFUL HEARTS

"The human heart is the most deceitful of all things,
and desperately wicked.
Who really knows how bad it is?
But I, the LORD, search all hearts
and examine secret motives.
I give all people their due rewards,
according to what their actions deserve."
– Jeremiah 17:9-10

As most parents of toddlers can attest, our sweet little babies quickly show us that though still tiny, they can throw some pretty amazing tantrums. Some of it is simply a difference of opinion (no, I won't eat that!), but they can also start showing unkind behaviors toward others. Unfortunately, this doesn't really go away on its own as they get older and it's not hard to believe that Jeremiah 17:9 is true.

If there's any doubt, we have only to take a close look at our *own* hearts and face the messiness inside. If we're truly honest, we all have a tendency toward thoughts if not actions we would never want to admit. Even worse, our hearts seem to want to deceive us into believing things an objective perspective would show to be false.

It's easy to get trapped in wrong thinking. As brain researchers have shown scientifically, our brains have neuroplasticity, meaning they can change and literally rewire themselves based on our thought patterns.[v] If we let ourselves get into negative patterns of thinking, we can very quickly get stuck there without an intentional choice to change the way we think about something. That stuck thinking, in turn, can lead us into behavior patterns that can be tough to stop. We'll see that in this next passage about Judah.

Read Jeremiah 17:1-10. What stands out to you in the poetic imagery?

What contrast do you see between verses 5-6 and 7-8?

As we've seen earlier, the prophets use repetition to emphasize certain points. The second part of this passage has a clear link back to the psalm that opened the Kethuvim section of the Hebrew Bible, Psalm 1, which is printed below. As you read it, look for how it compares to Jeremiah 17:5-10.

> "Oh, the joys of those who do not
> > follow the advice of the wicked,
> > or stand around with sinners,
> > or join in with mockers.
> But they delight in the law of the LORD,
> > meditating on it day and night.
> They are like trees planted along the riverbank,
> > bearing fruit each season.
> Their leaves never wither,
> > and they prosper in all they do.
> But not the wicked!
> > They are like worthless chaff, scattered by the wind.
> They will be condemned at the time of judgment.
> > Sinners will have no place among the godly.
> For the LORD watches over the path of the godly
> > but the path of the wicked leads to destruction."

What similar words, phrases and images do you see between Psalm 1 and Jeremiah 17:5-10?

In theory, the people of Jeremiah's day should likely have recognized the parallels to Psalm 1. The people needed reminded of the blessings God would give His faithful followers: keeping them like a tree by a river, not bothered by heat or drought and producing fruit. The people of Judah had long since embraced thought patterns that did not include meditating on God's word and His truths. Jeremiah reminded them what their lives could look like if they renewed their minds.

Read Jeremiah 17:11-18. What link do you see to another passage we read yesterday? Why is Jeremiah feeling like he does?

As in Jeremiah 2, we see a charge in verse 13 that the people "have abandoned the LORD, the fountain of living water." We again see Jeremiah making a contrast between the way the people have chosen to live versus what God called them to do. The people mocked Jeremiah because they hadn't seen his prophecies come true. Jeremiah was ready for God to fulfill His words to show the people the messages truly came from Yahweh. The living water analogy also ties to the first part of Jeremiah 17 and Psalm 1. The tree planted by the river needed the river's life-giving water.

I feel for Jeremiah. It would be so hard to stay strong, following the LORD, while experiencing persecution. It's baffling to me why wicked people seem to prosper while others trying their best to obey God don't seem to gain anything by obedience. It makes me think of Job, which I just reread this week. Job saw that the wicked seemed to prosper despite their sinful behavior and he questioned God about it.

Read Job 21:4-9. Have you ever felt like Job in this passage? Or like Jeremiah wondering when God would do what He said? If so, in what way(s)?

It can be so discouraging to wait on the LORD. But, toward the end of Job, he received this response found in Job 38:1-7:

"Then the LORD answered Job from the whirlwind:
'Who is this that questions my wisdom
*   with such ignorant words?*
Brace yourself like a man,
*   because I have some questions for you,*
*   and you must answer them.*
'Where were you when I laid the foundations of the earth?
*   Tell me, if you know so much.*
Who determined its dimensions
*   and stretched out the surveying line?*
What supports its foundations,
*   and who laid its cornerstone*
as the morning stars sang together
*   and all the angels shouted for joy?'"*

In another link between passages, these words in Job 38 tie to Isaiah 40.

Read Isaiah 40:12-31 or if you have time, start at verse 1. Where do you see echoes of the LORD's words to Job in this passage?

What encouragement do you see for yourself or others who may be going through a hard time?

It's easy to become discouraged like Jeremiah and Job when we don't see where God is working in our lives. And yet, in the LORD's response to Job and again in this passage in Isaiah, it's clear there is much we don't understand. Isaiah reminds us how small we are in the grand scheme of things. And then shifting perspectives, the next section opens in reverse by having us look up toward heaven to see the grandeur of the night sky. As Isaiah 40:26 says,

> *"Look up into the heavens.*
> *Who created all the stars?*
> *He brings them out like an army, one after another,*
> *calling each by its name.*
> *Because of His great power and incomparable strength,*
> *not a single one is missing."*

We see a clear reminder here of God's sovereignty. I can't tell you how many times this verse has come to mind as I've been praying about something. God uses it to pull me back from my request to remember God is so much bigger, higher, and greater than what I can see. We saw a similar message in Isaiah 37:26 as Isaiah prophesied about Assyria. God plans and allows things for a time, but He remains in control.

As the passage goes on in verse 27, it seems to speak so clearly to Job, Jeremiah, and even us today as we bring cares and concerns to the LORD. It can feel like He's not doing what He should, like He isn't taking care of us the way He would if He truly loved us. But again, this passage takes us beyond our concerns of the moment to remind us God is everlasting. He is the timeless Creator of the world who never grows weak and tired.

And even in whatever our circumstances may be, this passage reminds us He will give us strength to carry on when we put our trust in Him. The promise isn't victory or that things will turn out the way we want. Instead, it reminds us that God offers us something different in place of cracked cisterns that won't fill us.

> Where do you find yourself on the spectrum of trusting the LORD? Are there areas where you've abandoned the living water? What may God be asking you to do?

PRAYER FOCUS

As we close, spend time meditating on any passages from today that stood out to you. Thank the LORD for what He's been doing in your situation even if you don't see it.

Is there anything you need to confess or surrender?

Have you, like Job, been impatient with God? While God ultimately vindicated Job (see Job 42:7-17), much of the LORD's response to Job sounds like a reproach. Job responded humbly (see Job 40:3-5 and 42:1-6) and the LORD sees our hearts.

THE POTTER AND THE CLAY

"The LORD gave another message to Jeremiah. He said, "Go down to the potter's shop, and I will speak to you there." So I did as he told me and found the potter working at his wheel. But the jar he was making did not turn out as he had hoped, so he crushed it into a lump of clay again and started over."
– Jeremiah 18:1-4

When I was in first grade, my older brother and I started taking piano lessons from my classmate's mom. Besides teaching piano, my instructor and her husband owned a local pottery shop in our small town in northwestern Illinois. I remember going to visit the pottery shop and watching as Mr. Eshelman demonstrated how to use a potter's wheel to transform a lump of clay into a clearly shaped item. He made it look so easy!

As I read our passage for today, I can't help but imagine a scene like the one in the small-town shop of my childhood. The potter, focused on his work, has his hands messy from molding the wet clay. As you read, try to picture what Jeremiah describes.

Read Jeremiah 18:1-5. How does the pottery imagery illustrate what God planned and why?

In the opening lines, God gave Jeremiah a specific assignment and told him He would speak to Jeremiah once he went where God told him to go, to the potter's house. This reminds me God often only shows us His plan bit by bit. He'll ask us to do something and once we've obeyed him and it's time, He'll show us the next step.

Have you seen that in your own life? If so, how and when?

Read Jeremiah 18:5-17. As you think about your own life, are there any areas where it seems like God may be breaking something you didn't want broken?

As Jeremiah watched the potter work, he saw the item in progress get spoiled, so the potter took the same clay and started over. The clay wasn't new, but as he started his work again, the vessel was. Just as the potter had started over when the clay got spoiled, God has the power to tear down an entire nation if it, too, becomes spoiled, evil, rebellious. He offered once again that Judah could repent of its sin and turn back to the LORD, but the people refused to turn from the plans of their stubborn hearts.

And so, God was about to allow Judah to be destroyed because of its idolatry. They had stumbled from the ancient paths, turning from the highway to walk down a side path. While the potter's original plan wasn't to destroy the vessel he started, it reached a point where the clay needed a fresh start. In a similar way, the state of things in Judah had strayed far from Yahweh's path. So, the LORD, like the potter, was about to do something drastic because of how off-track His creation, His people, had gone. Even as the LORD told Jeremiah of the coming fall of Jerusalem, God asked him to do something surprising.

Read Jeremiah 32:1-8.

By this point, Jerusalem lay under siege. Because we know it fell to the Babylonians in King Zedekiah's 11th year, this happened shortly before the promised destruction came. Yet, with Jerusalem on the verge of disaster, God told Jeremiah to buy a field of all things. And this was while Jeremiah himself was a prisoner because he faithfully told the people what God said even though it angered the king.

How did Jeremiah know God had spoken to him?

Read Jeremiah 32:9-25. Why did God tell Jeremiah to buy the field and how does he seem to feel about the land purchase?

I would guess Jeremiah didn't have much money and this purchase sounds like a waste with the Babylonians about to overrun the land. What good would it do for him to own a field if an enemy nation took over?

Why do you think Jeremiah recounts Israel's exodus from Egypt in his prayer? Do you recognize what he's quoting in verse 18?

In his prayer, Jeremiah described Yahweh using the same words the LORD used to describe His own character back in Exodus 34:7. He also recalled God's past faithfulness in bringing the Israelites out of slavery in Egypt. In looking back at how God came through for His people during an earlier pivotal time in their history, Jeremiah seems to be reminding himself that God could do the same again. Indeed, trusting in God's sovereign character may have been the only way Jeremiah could make sense of what the LORD told him to do.

Can you think of a time when God has told you something that seemed odd or made you question if it was really God? How did you know it was?

If you look back over your past walk with the LORD like Jeremiah did with Israel's history, can you see how God's past faithfulness ties into what He's doing now? Why or why not?

Jeremiah 32:13-15 tell us the reason God had Jeremiah take this unlikely step. Just as the spoiled pottery was an image of the brokenness of Judah, the land purchase was a symbol of what was to come like the newly reformed pottery vessel. It wasn't to come for a long time, but there would be a day when God would bring His people back to the land He had promised them—promised to *Abraham* back in Genesis 12. They would once more buy and sell land just as Jeremiah had purchased the field. Judgment for sin was coming, but God already had a restoration plan in the works. And that is exactly what we see in the passages that follow (see Jeremiah 32:26-33:26).

It's encouraging to see that even while Jerusalem was under siege and about to fall, God was already looking out for their future welfare. And sometimes that will mean He asks us to do something with eyes of faith just like He did with Jeremiah. We must trust that while obedience doesn't look practical in the moment, He will bring blessing from it even if it takes years or decades before it's fulfilled. Or perhaps not seen this side of heaven.

Are there any areas where He seems to be asking you to do something that really doesn't make sense in light of your present circumstances?

PRAYER FOCUS

Spend time in prayer, thanking God for what He's doing in your life, listening for any direction He may have for you, and confessing any ways you've hesitated to obey. Is the LORD asking you to step out in faith, believing that even if you don't see the result for a long time, He will accomplish what concerns you as it says in Psalm 138:8?

DAY 5

REDEEMING THE YEARS

"The LORD says, "I will give you back what you lost
to the swarming locusts, the hopping locusts,
the stripping locusts, and the cutting locusts.
It was I who sent this great destroying army against you."
– Joel 2:25

Have you ever gone through a terrible season that seemed completely not worthwhile? I know for myself, when I can at least find a bright side to something difficult it can take a bit of the edge off a tough situation. But, when I can't see any way that something could possibly be good, it can be hard to reconcile. Especially when that season may last for years, or the rest of a lifetime.

I've been thinking about that a lot this last week after the sudden and untimely death of a friend. He was one of those people who exuded joy and drew people to him. While only 39, he left behind a wife of 18 years and three children age 13 and younger. He also left behind quite a legacy of lives impacted by his time here on earth, but I can't help but wonder why he wasn't given more years to impact more people. And what about his wife and kids who must navigate his loss for the rest of their lives? What good comes out of a permanent loss like that?

What we're going to read today made me think about that even more. The people Joel addressed had brought calamity upon themselves by turning away from God so it might be easy for us to blame the situation on them and move on. We also are unlikely to deal with the exact same troubles they faced so that can make it hard to relate, too. But if you look past the warning and judgment for their specific sins, the message of hope despite those hard times still resonates now.

Read Joel 1. As you read, look for familiar phrases or themes connected to other passages we've read or that you already know and jot them down below.

The opening verse doesn't give us much context for who Joel was besides his father's name, and no specific kings or dates are mentioned in the whole book.

While it's possible Joel lived during the Assyrian empire, some scholars think this message was to Judah just before a Babylonian invasion or after the exile ended.[vi]

As Joel describes the devastation from the locusts, we see a similar picture to what we read in Habakkuk 3:17-19 printed below.

> *"Even though the fig trees have no blossoms,*
> *and there are no grapes on the vines;*
> *even though the olive crop fails,*
> *and the fields lie empty and barren;*
> *even though the flocks die in the fields,*
> *and the cattle barns are empty,*
> *yet I will rejoice in the LORD!*
> *I will be joyful in the God of my salvation!*
> *The Sovereign LORD is my strength!*
> *He makes me as surefooted as a deer,*
> *able to tread upon the heights."*

Remember back in session one where we talked about how the twelve books we refer to as the Minor Prophets were all written on one scroll? Five minor prophet books were in between Joel and Habakkuk, but anyone who was familiar with the scroll with the twelve books would likely have seen the connection between Joel 1 and Habakkuk 3. And while both describe times of great lack, Habakkuk reminds us that even in those difficult times, God would always be faithful.

Joel 1 also includes a parallel to Zephaniah 1, the chapter immediately after Habakkuk 3. Zephaniah, like Joel, describes the day of the LORD as a time of devastation and ruin. Both also follow these warnings with calls to repentance.

What does Joel call the people to do in light of the bleak picture he described?

Joel told the people to fast, have a solemn assembly, and cry out to the LORD. Like Habakkuk, he knew the troubles they experienced didn't mean God wasn't able to help. Instead, their hardships should have been a reminder to turn back to the LORD.

Read Joel 2:1-17. How does this passage build on Joel 1? What does he tell the people to do?

Reread verses 12-14; how does Joel describe the LORD? Where have you seen this before?

We have another link back to Exodus 34 here, which connects to other passages we've read, too. Then, Joel builds on that with another message of hope.

Read Joel 2:18-27. What hope does Joel offer to the people even in spite of the locusts? How does this contrast with Joel 1:10-12 and Habakkuk 3:17-19?

Here Joel promises that God would intervene and restore His people if they turned back to Him. He would give back what was lost.

Thinking of the locusts, can you relate to the devastation Joel describes, perhaps from a great heartache, lonely season, family crisis, or poor health? Why or why not?

Have you seen God redeem or make up for those times, even years? Or are you still waiting?

For me, many of the seasons that left me feeling devastated included prolonged periods of waiting. And what often made the waiting even harder was knowing God could have intervened, but for reasons I couldn't understand at the time, didn't seem to be doing anything. In His grace, I can look back with hindsight and see His hand at work, weaving together pieces I didn't recognize at the time and building my personal character. Looking back at God's past faithfulness when I couldn't see it gives me hope as I wrestle through new challenges and unknowns today.

As we wait and struggle through the hard times Joel describes, Habakkuk seems to have discovered the key that makes all the difference. He shows us a better way as he committed to rejoicing and being joyful in the LORD even when circumstances seemed bleak. He reaffirmed that God was His salvation and strength even in hardship. When we don't have that kind of mindset, it can feel like a monumental task to renew how we think, but what a difference it can make when we do! It reminds me of what the apostle Paul wrote to the Ephesians centuries after both Joel and Habakkuk's lifetimes.

Read Ephesians 4:17-24. How does Paul describe the minds of those who don't follow God?

What does Paul tell Christians to do instead?

Not much has changed between the behavior the prophets condemned and how the people of Ephesus lived. Paul paints a clear contrast between the minds and thoughts of the non-believing people and the ones who followed God. Instead of letting popular culture guide them, Paul challenged those who followed Jesus to set aside their former way of living that had been corrupted by lust and deception. Instead, He told them to let their thoughts and attitudes be renewed by the Holy Spirit. This process would help them become more like God, holy and righteous.

How have you seen this in your own life?

It can feel like no good can possibly come out of a hard season. Yet, I truly believe if we allow God to work in us during those times, He will redeem them even if it takes years or decades before we see it. As King David wrote in Psalm 27:11-14 many years ago,

"Teach me how to live, O LORD.
Lead me along the right path,
for my enemies are waiting for me.
Do not let me fall into their hands.
For they accuse me of things I've never done;
with every breath they threaten me with violence.
Yet I am confident I will see the LORD's goodness

while I am here in the land of the living.
Wait patiently for the LORD.
   Be brave and courageous.
   Yes, wait patiently for the LORD."

PRAYER FOCUS

Spend time in prayer, asking the LORD to reveal to you whether your mind needs renewed in any way. Have you experienced or are you still going through trauma or difficulty that makes it hard to see beyond your situation? Ask Him to open your eyes to anything you haven't seen and point out any thought patterns that are ultimately keeping you stuck.

All Nations

If the living water analogy we read about in Jeremiah sounds familiar, Jesus used this same imagery in John 4:1-26 as He talked to a woman in the region of Samaria. Remember the significance of Samaria earlier in our study? It was once the capital of the Northern Kingdom of Israel, but Assyria exiled its inhabitants. Those who remained intermarried with foreigners. Because of this mixed ethnicity and religious differences, the Jews of Jesus' day, descendants of the people of Judah in Jeremiah's time, looked down on people from Samaria.

The Jewish people of New Testament times saw God's blessing tied to their heritage. They seemed to have missed how God gave messages to other nations through prophets we've looked at like Jeremiah, Jonah and Nahum. Going even further back, they ignored what God told Abraham centuries earlier when He promised to make him and his descendants into a great nation in Genesis 12:1-3, which says:

> "The LORD had said to Abram, "Leave your native country, your relatives, and your father's family, and go to the land that I will show you. I will make you into a great nation. I will bless you and make you famous, and you will be a blessing to others. I will bless those who bless you and curse those who treat you with contempt. All the families on earth will be blessed through you."

Even in the beginning, God's promise to set apart Abraham's family and make them great came tied to a promise to bless *all* people through them. God's plan never changed even though the people lost sight of His heart for all nations. Jesus reiterated that message in John 4 as He offered hope to someone rejected by both the Jews and her own people.

If you have time, read John 4:27-42 where we see the Samaritan woman telling others about Jesus. Unlike Jeremiah's listeners who heard the message of hope and did not seem to give it much credence, the Samaritans who encountered Jesus believed the truth. As I think about what this all means for me today, I wonder—am I more like the people of Judah who refused to accept God's offer or more like the Samaritan woman who, sinner though she was, encountered Jesus in such a way that she couldn't wait to tell others about the hope He offered her?

Before getting together, have everyone complete Session 4.

1.   Open in prayer.

2.   Questions for the group:

- Have you had or do you now have any area(s) where God has given you a "vision for an appointed time"? What helps you wait well on the right time?

- What broken cisterns do you see people relying on instead of seeking the LORD? Why?

- Have you noticed areas where your own heart deceives you?

- In what ways does God remind you He's in control?

- Where has God asked you to do something surprising or unexpected? Do you know why, or not yet?

- Have you seen a time where the LORD revealed one step at a time as you followed Him by faith? When and how?

- Where have you seen God redeem lost years, lost time? Or if you haven't yet seen the redemption, is there an area where you can watch for how He might do that as you continue to wait?

Babylonian Dominance

SESSION 5
BEAUTY FOR ASHES

THE NEW COVENANT

"Put all your rebellion behind you, and find yourselves a new heart and a new spirit. For why should you die, O people of Israel? I don't want you to die, says the Sovereign LORD. Turn back and live!"
– Ezekiel 18:31-32

Have you ever been on the sidelines of watching something awful unfold in someone else's life but been powerless to stop it? It can be harder to recognize those situations in our own lives in a timely manner, but we can often see someone else's life a bit more objectively. Yet, by simple virtue of being more outside of the situation, we may not have any way to do much beyond trying to point out what's happening.

Today we're going to see that sort of dynamic as we look at the final four kings of Judah who came after Josiah. If you have time, read 2 Kings 23:29-24:20. Otherwise, here's a quick synopsis of the powers at play in the region during that time.

Over the 11.5 years following King Josiah's death, Judah had three kings named Jehoahaz, Jehoiakim, and Jehoiachin. The first two were Josiah's sons, but Jehoahaz only reigned 3 months before Egypt deposed him, took him off to Egypt, and installed his brother Jehoiakim in his place. Jehoiakim paid tribute to Egypt until 605 BC when history tells us Babylon defeated the Assyrians and Egyptians.[i]

As Babylon's army moved through Judah to challenge the retreating Egyptian army, King Jehoiakim pledged loyalty to Babylon until they reached a stalemate with Egypt in 601 BC at which point he switched his loyalty back to Egypt.[ii] Once King Nebuchadnezzar of Babylon had rebuilt his army, he came against Jerusalem in 598 BC.[iii] Jehoiakim seems to have been killed and while his teenage son Jehoiachin took his place, the latter surrendered to Babylon three months later. Nebuchadnezzar took Jehoiachin and 10,000 people captive to Babylon.[iv] While Jeremiah was left in Jerusalem, Ezekiel was one of the captives who went into exile.

Once in Babylon, God called Ezekiel to prophesy to the others taken captive with him. During the early part of his ministry, Jerusalem had not yet fallen and was ruled by the final of Josiah's sons to reign, Zedekiah.

Read Ezekiel 18. What overarching theme do you see in this chapter?

Ezekiel makes it clear that while the people might think they were being punished unfairly, they were each accountable for their own behavior. God was willing to forgive anyone who repented, but His justice required a punishment, death, for those who did not repent. At the end, though, we see again that God doesn't want to punish anyone. We're going to see a similar message in Jeremiah starting with a promise of hope.

Read Jeremiah 31:15-30. How does this relate to Ezekiel 18? What hope do you see for yourself?

Jeremiah includes the same quote as Ezekiel and similar imagery to Joel, Habakkuk, Isaiah, and Hosea. Again, we see a promise not only for the people returning to their land, but also of future blessing beyond that. Verses 36-37 echo Jeremiah 33:25-26.

Jeremiah paints a picture of the people as God's children. He longs for their return as a father waits for His wayward children to come back home. To help them get back to Him, He tells them in Jeremiah 31:20-22 to set up signs and guideposts to mark the way.

Read Jeremiah 31:31-40. What distinguishes the new covenant from the old one?

Getting to the heart of the matter in verses 31-34, Yahweh promised a day when He would make a new covenant with His people. It had become woefully obvious they could not keep the existing covenant through Moses, and we see that acknowledged here. Jeremiah 31:32b tells us Yahweh "loved them as a husband loves his wife," but the people still broke the covenant in spite of that love.

Unlike the previous covenant with external commandments to follow, God promised to put His instructions deep inside each person, writing them on their hearts. Highlight or underline what stands out to you in Jeremiah 31:35-37 printed below:

> "It is the LORD who provides the sun to light the day
>   and the moon and stars to light the night,
>   and who stirs the sea into roaring waves.
> His name is the LORD of Heaven's Armies,
>   and this is what he says:
> "I am as likely to reject my people Israel
>   as I am to abolish the laws of nature!"
> This is what the LORD says:
> "Just as the heavens cannot be measured
>   and the foundations of the earth cannot be explored,
> so I will not consider casting them away
>   for the evil they have done.
>   I, the LORD, have spoken!"

What a powerful assurance! Yahweh would warn them to turn from their wickedness and bring judgment on the people for their unrepentant hearts. But completely give up on them? Absolutely not.

Spend some time reflecting on the passage above. What stands out to you? Thinking about your life today, where do these promises offer you encouragement?

Because God's character never changes, we can trust these promises still stand today as well. God has written His law on our hearts just as He promised. We're also going to circle back to Joel one more time.

Read Joel 2:28-32. How does this passage add to what Jeremiah wrote about the new covenant?

Now, **read Acts 2:14-21.** How does this relate to what we just read in Joel?

This time, we see the new covenant wasn't just for the Israelites, but for *all* people including both men and women, and even servants. He doesn't want any to perish, no matter who they are. His never stopping, endless love is for anyone. Because He is just and holy, the new covenant offers a way to be made right with God without a need to follow commands we can't keep on our own. At the same time, our sins would bear the price of death. In the end, God chose to satisfy that price by sending Jesus to be our Savior.

What stood out to you the most in the passages we read today? Why?

Praise God for this new covenant and sending Jesus to take our penalty on Himself!

PRAYER FOCUS

Spend time in prayer, confessing any ways your actions don't line up with how God wants us to live. Ask Him to open your eyes to anything you don't see that you may need to repent of. And thank Him for accepting all of us, no matter what, because of His unfailing love.

DAY 2

SEEKING THE PEACE OF THE CITY

"This is what the LORD says: 'You will be in Babylon for seventy years. But then I will come and do for you all the good things I have promised, and I will bring you home again. For I know the plans I have for you,' says the LORD. 'They are plans for good and not for disaster, to give you a future and a hope. In those days when you pray, I will listen. If you look for me wholeheartedly, you will find me. I will be found by you,' says the LORD. 'I will end your captivity and restore your fortunes. I will gather you out of the nations where I sent you and will bring you home again to your own land.'"
– Jeremiah 29:10-14

If I tell my daughters we're going to the park or to their grandparents' house, or that they can have a piece of candy, they won't forget. They do seem a little fuzzy on the timing, though. So, if I tell them we'll go to Grammie and Grandpa's house tomorrow, they want to go *now*. Waiting a day seems far too long so I don't give them too much notice about most things.

I've had some pretty humbling moments myself where God has shown me I'm waiting on His timing just as impatiently as my little girls wait on mine. When He helps me see what I'm doing, I try to remind myself to treasure those things in my heart while not yet understanding the bigger picture. It can feel really tough when time continues to pass, though. It makes me wonder if I misunderstood what I thought God told me He was going to do.

One of the most significant of these for me personally had to do with some specific things I felt God impress on my heart about the person I would marry. As time went on and He continued to whisper *no* in my heart to potential guys who seemed to fit one part or another of what He had shown me, I began to question whether I was crazy and completely wrong. But then, when I was dating my now husband, as I prayed for wisdom, God brought all those prior promises to mind and showed me one by one how this guy fit *all* of them, even down to his name, Joseph.

What God didn't tell me in advance, though, was the timing. And to be honest, if He had said it would be seven years before I saw His answer fulfilled, I probably would have felt resistant. Instead, because I *didn't* know, I kept pressing in and trusting even when it got confusing and seemed like I had missed something along the way. Believing God felt especially hard at different points of the journey, but in His perfect timing, He did what He said.

Even better, I can look back and see how the timing was truly what it needed to be. I had things to learn during that time that would have been far harder with a family. And my husband, too, had things he was working through. If we had met around the time God gave me glimpses of what was to come, neither of us would have been the person the other was looking for. We both had transforming to do during that time of waiting.

This will tie into our reading today, but I also share this story because I know many of you may be in a similar space of waiting for something and wondering if God has forgotten you. Wondering if God really said what He did. Feeling sad, discouraged, or even a little bitter about God's timing. You may have waited longer than I did and your season may be far more painful than mine, but please know you are not forgotten.

Have you had a time where God told you something you struggled to believe? What made it difficult and have you seen His word fulfilled?

We sometimes have to hold onto what God has said and while not forgetting, press into a time of not seeing how everything ties together. Waiting, but still full of faith. The prophets likely had to do the same thing, especially when time passed and God didn't bring the judgment He told them would come. That is what we find Jeremiah calling the exiles to do during their time in Babylon.

Read Jeremiah 29:1-23. Who is the letter to and what is its context?

What does he tell them to do and why?

I think Jeremiah 29:11 may be one of the verses I've heard quoted out of context more than any other verse. Yes, it's very encouraging and hopeful, but the rest of the passage is so critical for really understanding the intent. Jeremiah who still lived in Jerusalem wrote this letter to the people of Judah already exiled to Babylon. As verse 19 makes clear, these exiles weren't listening to God's word through his true prophets anymore than their countrymen back in Judah.

In the last session, we read Jeremiah 18 that talked about the potter and the clay. Look at Jeremiah 29:11 and then see how it compares to Jeremiah 18:11 printed below.

> *"Therefore, Jeremiah, go and warn all Judah and Jerusalem. Say to them, 'This is what the LORD says: I am planning disaster for you instead of good. So turn from your evil ways, each of you, and do what is right.'"*

Jeremiah uses some of the same words and phrases in both verses, but pointing to different outcomes. To the people still in Judah and Jerusalem, he proclaimed God's plans for them would bring disaster, not good. To the people already exiled to Babylon, he spoke of God's plans to give them good, not disaster.

Why do you think God's planned good for one group and not for the other?

In both places, Jeremiah points to God's sovereignty even over nations. God had promised disaster for Judah's sins and He had not yet fulfilled His word. Yet, for those already exiled, God sent a reminder through Jeremiah's letter that He had not given up on His people even though they had been forced from their land.

Along with the message of hope came a clear reminder that they wouldn't return home soon. False prophets had been saying the exile would be short, but Jeremiah wrote to tell them God had said it would last 70 years. Thinking of an average lifetime, most of the exiles would not live long enough to return to their homeland.

In the midst of this time of waiting, verses 4-7 seem striking. God told them to live full lives during their time in exile. They weren't to pine away, live in tents, or refuse to have families. Instead, they were to build houses and plant gardens to feed themselves. He told them to marry and have children. Rather than putting their lives on hold as they waited, God called them to live their best lives even though they weren't where they wanted to be.

What did God specifically tell them to do regarding the city of Babylon and why was this surprising?

Instead of viewing Babylon as a horrible place, a terrible season in their history and wanting to see bad things happen to it, God told them to seek its welfare. To *work* for its peace and prosperity. This wasn't an idle, passive statement where they could sit by and watch what happened, but instead, they were to get involved in making Babylon a better place to live. In doing so, their own welfare would improve along with the city's.

Seeing Babylon in this way called them to renew their thinking about this enemy city that had turned their lives upside down. God sent them there for a time period He set and He essentially told them to cooperate with Him. This makes me think of Zephaniah 3:5, which we read earlier in this study:

> *"But the LORD is still there in the city,*
> *and he does no wrong.*
> *Day by day he hands down justice,*
> *and he does not fail.*
> *But the wicked know no shame."*

While this prophecy was talking about Jerusalem, the heart of it seems to apply regardless of the specific location. Good, bad, in between—God was present in Jerusalem and He would be with them in Babylon as well. We see an example of someone who did just what Jeremiah said, although it's not clear whether Daniel saw Jeremiah's letter before it's mentioned in Daniel 9:1-2 or not. As we read this next chapter, look for how Daniel lived out what Jeremiah wrote to the exiles to do.

Read Daniel 1. How did Daniel and his three friends react to the role the Babylonians assigned them?

This chapter introduces us to four young men who were taken captive from Judah to Babylon and trained to serve the king. While it might have been easy to feel angry with their captors and try to resist, undermine, or outright sabotage what these foreign oppressors wanted them to do, these four young men didn't do that. They stood up for what they knew was right, but in a respectful way and God gave them favor with the chief of staff.

What did the king of Babylon look for in these young men and what was the outcome?

We can learn a lot from these men about remaining faithful while not compromising our convictions. In today's day and age, the internet allows people to quickly share their thoughts about leaders and policies, but not necessarily in a respectful way. Many people stand up for their beliefs, but in ways that divide rather than unite. King Nebuchadnezzar of Babylon was someone these young men from Judah had good reason to dislike and speak against, but they provided "wisdom and balanced judgment" significantly above that of the king's own wise men.

As these men lived out what Jeremiah encouraged all the exiles to do, to promote the welfare of the place where they now lived, we can find an example of how we, too, should live. We don't have to agree with everyone to promote peace. We don't have to *like* everyone to still seek their welfare. Even if it feels like wisdom gets ignored, if we are committed to being people who speak and behave in ways that reflect wisdom, others will notice even if it doesn't seem like it. We all are influencers in our own spheres, however large or small. Even as we should stick to our convictions, we should also exemplify wise, respectful behavior.

Thinking about your own life, are there any areas where you have backed down from standing for your convictions?

Or are there ways you've taken a stand, but in a way that didn't reflect wisdom? We can be right about something, but the value can be lost if we communicate about it in unhelpful ways.

Are there ways that you may need to seek forgiveness for the way you've handled a disagreement or how you stood up for what you think is right?

PRAYER FOCUS

Thinking about all these things, ask the LORD to reveal any change you may need to make or to encourage you in areas where you need to stand strong. It's a tricky time for navigating different views, but it was no less challenging in Daniel's day even without social media. Jot down anything that comes to mind as you pray.

CONFESSION AND RENEWAL

"I prayed to the LORD my God and confessed: 'O Lord, you are a great and awesome God! You always fulfill your covenant and keep your promises of unfailing love to those who love you and obey your commands. But we have sinned and done wrong. We have rebelled against you and scorned your commands and regulations. We have refused to listen to your servants the prophets, who spoke on your authority to our kings and princes and ancestors and to all the people of the land.'"
– Daniel 9:4-6

In the first month or two of the Covid-19 pandemic, I felt a great burden to pray for my nation and people around the world. I had already been studying the topic of confession and wondered if God had allowed this illness to spread so quickly in so many places because we as a collective society have turned away from Him in many ways. I don't know the answer to that, but it did remind me of the importance of regularly examining my heart and confessing sin. This next passage we're going to read speaks to that.

Read Daniel 9:1-23. What stands out to you in Daniel's prayer?

What prompted Daniel to pray as he did? What did Daniel ask God to do? What was his hope?

What happened after Daniel's prayer?

I find this prayer incredibly moving. Daniel lived a faithful life to God, standing up for what was right even while surrounded by very powerful people. He was given great authority himself, as well. And yet, here we see him grouping himself with his people who had *not* been faithful. He confessed their collective sins against God, recounting God's character and the history of how they came to be exiled. Toward the end, he pled with Yahweh for His own sake to grant them favor again and restore ruined Jerusalem.

As I thought about why Daniel asked God to act for His own sake, it reminded me of what Moses had said when Yahweh wanted to destroy the people in the wilderness for their disobedience. Moses, like Daniel, appealed to God's character and begged Him to forgive His wayward people. And God did, which is when He gave the Exodus 34 description of Himself to Moses. Daniel clearly knew the history of his nation and believed that God would grant his plea because Daniel, like Moses, knew God's character.

And the really amazing part of this to me is how God answered Daniel with a visit from the angel Gabriel! If you finish Daniel 9, you'll see the specifics of what Gabriel told him, but this part in verses 20-23 makes me cry:

> *"I went on praying and confessing my sin and the sin of my people, pleading with the LORD my God for Jerusalem, his holy mountain. As I was praying, Gabriel, whom I had seen in the earlier vision, came swiftly to me at the time of the evening sacrifice. He explained to me, "Daniel, I have come here to give you insight and understanding. The moment you began praying, a command was given. And now I am here to tell you what it was, for you are very precious to God. Listen carefully so that you can understand the meaning of your vision."*

Not only did God send an angel to give Daniel "insight and understanding," but it says *"the moment you began praying, a command was given."* Even though Daniel didn't *get* the answer with his first word, God had sent one. It reminds me the LORD knows what we're going to pray before we even say the words, and that He is outside of time. We can also be confident that when we're confessing sin, God hears us and is faithful to forgive. When we pray in alignment with His will—and confessing our sin always fits that category—then we can know beyond a shadow of a doubt that He hears us.

He sees our hearts and knew Daniel was sincere. If we pray words of confession but with hearts that are still far from God or don't mean what we say, He knows that. Sincere confession will come with repentance, turning away from our sinful behavior. We've seen again and again how God promises to show mercy to those who repent. From deserving death, He gives us life.

I love how one of Ezekiel's visions illustrates this as well giving a further glimpse of how God would answer Daniel's prayer and those of others who were faithful.

Read Ezekiel 37:1-14. What stands out to you in this passage?

This passage gives me so much hope as it shows God can bring life out of what looks completely, irrevocably dead. And even more than being a picture of how God would restore Israel, it also mirrors the new covenant where those who believe in Jesus have been made alive through Him.

Read Ephesians 2:1-10. What similarities do you see between how Daniel and the apostle Paul describe God's character?

How does Ephesians compare to what we read in Ezekiel?

Read Ezekiel 37:15-28. How does this passage build on the vision of the dry bones?

What hope does this give us today?

Here we see a promise that Israel and Judah would be reunited despite their division centuries before. Along with that, we see a promise of a new covenant of peace where God would again live in their midst. Just as we saw in Jeremiah 31:27-40, God had already made a way for His people to be restored long before He made it happen. It reminds me again of how Daniel's prayer got an immediate answer even though he didn't see it right away.

Thinking back over what we've just read, can you think of any areas where you may need to pray a confession, whether for yourself, another group you're in, your nation, or something else? Are there areas where you've nearly given up hope because it seems like the situation is just as dead as the valley of dry bones? Spend time praying as you feel led and jot down anything that comes to mind in the space below.

DAY 4

THEN ALL WILL KNOW

"Then I will sprinkle clean water on you, and you will be clean. Your filth will be washed away, and you will no longer worship idols. And I will give you a new heart, and I will put a new spirit in you. I will take out your stony, stubborn heart and give you a tender, responsive heart. And I will put my Spirit in you so that you will follow my decrees and be careful to obey my regulations."
– Ezekiel 36:25-27

When we're in the middle of something, it can be hard to see too far beyond the present. Looking back at my junior high years, they felt like forever and things seemed so important that I don't care about one bit today. And there are things that didn't seem to matter then that I know now matter very much. My perspective shifts as I continue learning and experiencing new things.

I have a hard time wrapping my mind around how God can be outside of time and know the future in advance. Yet, because He knows what's coming, He can give us a glimpse of things before they happen. As we read this next passage, think about what Jeremiah's listeners might have thought as they heard his prophecy of what was to come.

> **Read Jeremiah 50:1-20.** For those who believed Jeremiah's prophecy, what might they have expected to happen soon? What conclusion might they have if they didn't see it come true in the timing they expected?

This is toward the end of a section with messages to other nations that ends with promises of judgment on Babylon. Jeremiah sent this message to Babylon in 593 B.C. (see Jeremiah 51:59), about 7 years before Jerusalem fell in 586 B.C.[v]

For those who did believe Jeremiah but saw the rising power of the Babylonians, it could have made them wonder if this time Jeremiah had it wrong. And as the next few years passed leading to Jerusalem's fall to Babylon, it might have made them especially wonder. The reminder in verses 17-18 that God punished Assyria, though, might have been enough to give them hope that this prophesy against Babylon would also come true.

Just as God promised judgment on Assyria and Babylon for their treatment of His people, He also did the same toward smaller, neighboring nations as well. One example that mirrors Jeremiah 49:7-22 is in the very short book of Obadiah and echoed in Ezekiel. [vi]

> **Read Obadiah 1:10-16 and Ezekiel 36:1-5.** Why did God promise to destroy Edom?

If you're wondering how Edom was a close relative of Israel, the Edomites were the descendants of Esau, Jacob's twin brother. Jacob and Esau were the sons of Isaac and grandsons of Abraham. They had a troubled past, but God had revealed a glimpse of that to their mother, Rebekah, before they were even born (see Genesis 25:19-26). Here, centuries later, God promised to destroy Esau's descendants because of how they treated the descendants of Jacob when God punished them.

Babylon and Edom had both mistreated the people of Judah beyond what Yahweh had intended when He pronounced judgment on them. So, their oppressors who had benefited at others' expense would be overtaken themselves. And now, we're going to shift into Babylon where Ezekiel continues to speak God's words to those exiled there from Judah.

> **Read Obadiah 1:17-21 and Ezekiel 36:6-21.** In spite of their exile, their fallen homeland, and how their neighbors treated them, what did God plan to do for His people?

> **Read Ezekiel 36:22-38 and 39:21-29.** Why does God tell His people He'll end their exile? What would the Israelites and the other nations realize when God brought His people back from exile?

We've seen how the prophets' messages of warning and judgment often also had a third part, hope. These passages show that the hope would come from God's character, not their own worthiness. The exile wouldn't fundamentally change them or make them right with God in itself.

When God restored them, they couldn't keep their idolatry and sins. He promised to cleanse them, giving them a new, responsive heart and His Spirit. The prophets heard God's word and while we see an exception in Jonah, they did as He asked. Once God gave His Spirit to all people, we could all have the opportunity to hear His voice. We're still no more able to keep the old covenant than the people of the Old Testament but having the Holy Spirit would remind us how to live.

The messages of the prophets of future restoration and hope for Israel and Judah sound specific to those groups, especially when other messages proclaim complete destruction on other nations like Babylon and Edom. And yet, as we've seen, God offered hope beyond the family of Jacob. We all can have the new heart and spirit Ezekiel described because we have a merciful, holy God.

We're so blessed to be able to hear God's word through His Spirit. For me, this has never been through an audible voice, but through a still small voice in my heart. I've learned to pay attention to anything that comes to mind when I pray. If I ask God a question, I pause and wait to see if He'll show me anything. If you haven't experienced this, it might sound as unlikely as the future fall of Babylon did to Jeremiah's listeners, but Jesus promised His sheep would hear His voice and know it was Him.

How do you typically hear God speak to you? How can you be sure it's God's voice you're hearing?

If you're unsure whether something is really from God, you can know He'll never tell you something or ask you to do anything that violates His character. The more you seek the LORD, the more you'll know about Him in order to discern truth from lies. Once you start recognizing how He speaks to you, there's a good chance you'll realize you've been hearing it all along without knowing it was Him.

Into what areas of your life do you long to hear God speak?

Spend time praying as you feel led and write down anything that comes to mind as you pray.

DAY 5

ABOUNDING IN LOVE

"That is why the LORD says,
    "Turn to me now, while there is time.
Give me your hearts.
    Come with fasting, weeping, and mourning.
Don't tear your clothing in your grief,
    but tear your hearts instead."
Return to the LORD your God,
    for He is merciful and compassionate,
slow to get angry and filled with unfailing love.
    He is eager to relent and not punish.
Who knows? Perhaps He will give you a reprieve,
    sending you a blessing instead of this curse.
Perhaps you will be able to offer grain and wine
    to the LORD your God as before."
        – Joel 2:12-14

I sometimes make things harder for myself than they need to be. I remember trying to figure out what a teacher expected for an assignment and doing what seemed like the bare minimum only to realize the next day that others had done something far simpler and still met the requirements. On the flip side, when we know how to do something we can make it sound far easier than it really is. For example, as my husband recently tried to explain something to our oldest daughter, it sounded simple. For myself, though, I'd say it's much easier said than done.

In reading the passage above from Joel 2, I can see a bit of both sides of that dichotomy. On the one hand, because of God's compassion and love for us, repentance should be simple. But unfortunately, the turning away from the old ways that should come from true repentance may prove quite difficult. Growing up I was told it takes three weeks to break a habit. While that matches what I've read on brain research, it might feel a bit like swimming upstream if someone tries to make big changes without having a supportive community.[vii]

With that background in mind, **read Ezekiel 33:1-20.** How did God reiterate Ezekiel's calling and what would happen if Ezekiel disobeyed?

How did the people respond to Ezekiel's message?

Ezekiel was given a difficult task. People came to hear his words, but they seemed to have no intention of doing what he said. Yet, God made it clear that in his role as a watchman, Ezekiel would be held accountable for his own obedience in speaking God's words to the people. God didn't tell him to force people to change, but to speak the LORD's words to them regardless of the outcome.

Ezekiel knew what God had promised would happen if the people didn't repent. Remember how God had even told him back at the start of his ministry that the people wouldn't listen to him? It had to feel painful to see the train wreck coming, knowing the people were going to continue to experience God's judgment as they refused to turn from their sins. And yet, Ezekiel was faithful to God's call, even if it meant pressing into difficult realities.

Because mainstream Judean society had collectively strayed so far from Yahweh, the main times we've seen reformation came when a king did his best to lead the people back to the LORD. These kings used their power and influence to remove places of pagan worship and stop practices counter to God's word. Without such a king, the people went right back to the behavior he had tried to stop. And despite God's desire to bless the people, the day prophets had been warning would come, did in fact arrive.

Read Jeremiah 52:1-16. What tragedy do we see unfold in this passage?

Since Nebuchadnezzar had installed Zedekiah as king over Judah, he was supposed to stay loyal to Babylon. He did at first, but sometime before the ninth year of his reign, he rebelled, so Babylon began attacking Jerusalem on January 15, 588 BC.[viii] While the city was walled and they managed to withstand the siege for two and a half years, going through a severe famine to the point of running out of food, the city fell on August 14, 586 BC.[ix]

Read Ezekiel 33:21-33. How did the exiles respond to Ezekiel?

A few months after it happened, news of Jerusalem's fall reached Ezekiel in Babylon. People had scoffed at Jeremiah and other prophets as they kept announcing coming judgment, but it happened just as the prophets said it would. For anyone still holding false hope that the exile would be short, this would have finally made it clear they weren't going home soon. God continued speaking to the exiles through Ezekiel, calling them to repent where their countrymen back home had not. Sadly, they seem more entertained by Ezekiel than convicted of personal sin.

Even in the sorrow the people of Judah would have felt at the fall of Jerusalem, we've read prophecies in this session from Jeremiah, Obadiah, and Ezekiel that pointed the people toward a future hope. All may have seemed bleak, but God continued to let them know in advance what He planned to do to punish their oppressors and restore them. We see something similar from the prophet Joel.

Read Joel 3. What stands out to you in this chapter?

What hope does God offer His people even in their punishment? What encouragement does it give us today?

Again we see that God would punish nations who had harmed Yahweh's chosen people. It's disturbing to read some examples of that in the first part of the chapter. At the same time, I love how Joel closes with words of hope, of God's promised blessing. God did punish His people, but He didn't give up on them and He would still bring justice against the wicked. Because of who God is, He still loved them and His faithfulness didn't change as a result of the people's behavior. In light of that, Joel points us to the power of prayer.

Are there any areas of your life where you struggle to believe God has good in store for you? If so, what hope does Joel 3 give you?

The people of Judah could have believed they were too far gone for Yahweh to love and forgive them, but He still planned to even as they experienced consequences for their failure to turn back to Him. Ezekiel and Joel remind us it's never too late to seek the LORD and experience His mercy.

Don't lose heart! Keep praying and believing that our LORD is the same yesterday, today, and forever. He may not answer every prayer we ask in the way we hope, but we can be assured that as we bring our requests before Him, He hears us and will answer even if it's a no. Because of who He is, we can trust that even when He doesn't give us what we want, He never changes and will fulfill each of His promises to us. And so, let's keep praying, keep seeking Him, and keep centering our hearts on loving Him above all else. As the Scriptures promise, those who seek Him will find Him!

PRAYER FOCUS

Ask the LORD to show you if there are any areas of your life where you struggle to believe He has compassion for you. Have you believed any lies about His character? Do you believe He can work good out of the messiest part of your story? If it helps, journal in the space below.

Before getting together, have everyone complete Session 5.

1.   Open in prayer.

2.   Questions for the group:

- What impact does knowing some of the geopolitical history have on how you read these books?

- What stands out to you between the old (Mosaic) covenant and the New Covenant mentioned by several of the prophets?

- Where might God be calling you to seek the peace of the city, to live well exactly where you are whether you want to be there or not?

- Where do you see God at work in your life, even in unexpected places?

- If you were to pray and confess the sins of your people, whatever group or nation that might be, what would that include?

- What impact do you think confession could have on our relationship with God today, both on personal and corporate levels?

- Which aspect(s) of God's character stand out to you the most? Why?

- Are there any lies about who God is that you've struggled to overcome? Or are there areas where you struggle to see how God still offers you hope no matter your circumstances?

Persian Dominance

Session 6
The Remnant Returns

Day 1
Going Home

"I have refined you, but not as silver is refined.
Rather, I have refined you in the furnace of suffering.
I will rescue you for my sake—
yes, for my own sake!
I will not let my reputation be tarnished,
and I will not share my glory with idols!"
– Isaiah 48:10-11

Looking back over my journey so far, I can see how I've grown more in my faith and personal character from the challenges I've faced rather than in times that were smooth sailing. I certainly don't want to face difficulties, but experience has taught me to press in during those times and look for what God has to teach me. Often, hardship makes me face my own inadequacies and failures in a way that refines them and helps the lessons stick more. And perhaps this goes back to how our brains build connections—the situations that cause us to think harder and process more may cause the brain to grow in ways it wouldn't have.

Even as God allowed His people to experience the painful consequences of their rebellion against Him, He planned to use it for good. He wanted to break their habitual patterns of idolatry and selfishness, instead turning them back to the way He called them to live. Today we'll see a turning point in the story as the long Babylonian exile comes to an end.

Read Isaiah 48:1-11. Why did God tell the people what would happen in advance?

Yahweh told the people what would come so they would know it was Him who made it happen. Otherwise, they might have given credit to their idols rather than to the Creator. I also love how Isaiah 48:10 compares that process to refining silver. Just as heat can be used to purify silver, God used suffering to refine and purify His people and the same can be true for us today.

Read Isaiah 45:1-13 and 48:12-22. What does God tell them will happen?

Again, we see God telling them what was coming so when it happened, they'd know He was the one to do it. Through Isaiah, God told the people of Judah they'd return home and even named the future king who would conquer Babylon to replace that empire. He reminded them He is sovereign over all things, from nature to world kingdoms.

The end of Isaiah 48 also makes it clear that God's desire had been that they obey Him in the first place so they wouldn't need redeemed. Yet, He Himself would be their redeemer. Long before Judah was exiled to Babylon, God had already promised to bring them back to their land again. And when it was time, He did exactly that.

Read Ezra 1. What stands out to you in light of what we just read in Isaiah?

Persian King Cyrus and his Median counterpart, King Darius, took over Babylon in 539 B.C. Cyrus issued a decree allowing the Judeans to go home in 538 B.C.[i] I love how not only did God do what He promised by allowing them to go home, but He provided for their needs, too. Without extra financial help, it would have been difficult to rebuild, so He prompted King Cyrus to ask the neighbors of the Judean remnant to donate to them as they headed back to rebuild God's temple in Jerusalem.

This week, we'll focus on the hope in the prophetic message and how God fulfills His promises. We only have a few books post-exile and before we start reading in those, we're going to look at a couple more prophecies of future hope found in the book of Isaiah.

Read Isaiah 25:1-5. What repeated theme do you see here from what we've already read today?

Isaiah again points out how God plans things in advance and then makes them happen. He is sovereign over nations, but also a refuge for the poor and needy. Yahweh could calm the storms brought by the wicket.

Read Isaiah 25:6-9. What future promise does this include and who is it for?

We also see once again that the future hope would be for all people, not just the people of Israel and Judah. Death itself would be swallowed up forever and the LORD would wipe away all tears. However, the wicked and prideful would be punished.

Read Isaiah 26:1-13. Keeping in mind that God promised future hope for all peoples, what hope do you see in this passage for yourself? How can you lean into God's promise to keep those who trust in Him and who fix their thoughts on Him in "perfect peace"? Where have you seen that in your own life?

I went through a season where God pointed me back to Isaiah 26:3-4 repeatedly as I wrestled through some hard things. As I kept pressing in, I came to see how He gave me peace in the midst of the difficulties even when I couldn't see how they would change. The peace He gave wasn't dependent on my circumstances, but rather a gift in spite of them. While I don't do it perfectly, I've seen how fixing my thoughts on the LORD, seeking Him and trusting Him to provide have helped keep me steady in challenging situations. Isaiah's words weren't a trite platitude, but something we can still experience in our own lives today.

PRAYER FOCUS

Spend time reflecting and praising God for how you can see His hand at work in your life. Where do you need His perfect peace? Are there things you can release to Him, fixing your thoughts on Him rather than spiraling in negative or unhelpful thought patterns? Ask the LORD to give you eyes to see what He has for you.

DAY 2

REBUILDING THE RUINS

"But now the LORD says: Be strong, Zerubbabel. Be strong, Jeshua son of Jehozadak, the high priest. Be strong, all you people still left in the land. And now get to work, for I am with you, says the LORD of Heaven's Armies. My Spirit remains among you, just as I promised when you came out of Egypt. So do not be afraid.'"
– Haggai 2:4-5

Excitement can build momentum when something starts, but wane quickly when the hard realities of the daily grind set in. When I taught in a school setting, I always started the year excited, but within a month or two the exhaustion would kick in leaving me feeling drained and behind. The line between the workday and home got very blurry as there was always more to do.

I wonder if the people of Judah felt something similar after returning to Jerusalem. After living in exile, how excited they must have felt to go back under the good graces of the empire ruling their homeland. Seeing the ruined walls and temple must have felt overwhelming, but their initial excitement may have carried them for a while. Rebuilding would have required hard physical labor, though, and as it turned out, they also faced opposition from others living in the area.

As we read today, look for ways the prophetic message after the exile is similar or different to what we've seen before. Is there still warning of sin, a promise of judgment, and the promise of future hope?

> **Read Ezra 3:1-4:5.** Why do you think those who had seen the original Temple cried when they saw the foundation for the new Temple? Would you have felt the same? Why or why not?

Those who had seen the original Temple knew what a magnificent place it had been. It doesn't say for sure, but I imagine they felt a mixture of sadness at the loss of what was, sorrow at what had caused it, and deeply moved by their return. Those weeping were priests, Levites, and other leaders who likely knew God would have relented if they had heeded His warnings.

Read Ezra 4:24-5:1.

By the time we get to these verses, about 18 years have passed since King Cyrus allowed them to return to their homeland.[ii] After starting strong, the temple remained unfinished. And here we see mention of two of the few prophets who have books from the time of the Persian Empire, Haggai and Zechariah.

Read Haggai 1:1-11. What challenges were the people having and why did Haggai tell them they were experiencing these hardships?

While the work on the temple had paused, the remnant who returned had apparently built luxurious houses for themselves. Because they had allowed the Temple to stay in ruins, God sent a drought and prevented them from having a good harvest. Haggai warned them to change or they would lose all they had worked so hard to get.

Read Haggai 1:12-15. How did the people respond to Haggai's message?

Unlike their ancestors, these people took action in response to Haggai's warning and began rebuilding within a few weeks.

Read Haggai 2:1-9. What hope did the LORD promise?

Again, we see the new Temple did not match the original Temple's glory. Yet, Haggai encouraged them to stay strong and get the work done.

Read Haggai 2:10-19. What promise did Yahweh give them in advance?

What hope does Haggai 2 give us today?

Just as we've seen throughout this study, God calls everyone to live by His standards. While they were experiencing difficulties for their lack of obedience, Haggai reminded them that God would provide as they turned back to Him. We see a similar call from Haggai's peer, the prophet Zechariah.

> **Read Zechariah 1:1-17.** When was this message in relation to Haggai? What does Zechariah tell the people to do and how does this compare to the 3-part prophetic message of warning, judgment and then hope?

Despite the exile, we're starting to see some hints that the people's behavior may not have changed as much as we might have expected. For once, though, the leaders and others in the remnant who returned listened to Haggai and Zechariah when they challenged them to continue rebuilding the temple. These latter prophets still spoke of punishment for lack of repentance while offering hope for those who obeyed Yahweh.

> Are there any areas where you've grown weary in doing what God has asked you to do? What hope or encouragement has the LORD given you even if you're still in the middle of an exile of some sort or another?

PRAYER FOCUS

Thinking back over the seasons of your life so far, where have you seen God at work? Spend time thanking Him for what He has done so far. At the same time, where do you long to see Him do something? How can you lean into that and cooperate with what He may be doing? Pray as you feel led.

DAY 3

NOT BY EXILE ALONE

*"The L*ORD *of Heaven's Armies sent me this message in reply: "Say to all your people and your priests, 'During these seventy years of exile, when you fasted and mourned in the summer and in early autumn, was it really for me that you were fasting? And even now in your holy festivals, aren't you eating and drinking just to please yourselves? Isn't this the same message the L*ORD *proclaimed through the prophets in years past when Jerusalem and the towns of Judah were bustling with people, and the Negev and the foothills of Judah were well populated?'"*
– Zechariah 7:4-7

Have you ever wanted to change something, but found yourself returning to the same habits? Or decided to give something up for Lent only to forget and do the very thing you had decided to forgo? As we talked about before, the way we think can be very powerful and without changing those thought patterns, it can be tough to change our behavior. We're going to see that dynamic with the people of Zechariah's day.

Read Zechariah 7. What similarities do you see between what Zechariah charges the people with in this passage and earlier prophetic messages we've read?

What can you tell about their hearts from their question and Zechariah's answer about whether to keep fasting and mourning on the anniversary of the Temple's destruction?

Despite the joy of returning home and relief that the exile had ended, we see here a few years later that the exile didn't solve the underlying problems that caused it in the first place. But maybe that isn't so surprising given that God said He was bringing them back for His name's sake, not their own. They hadn't earned the right to return by good behavior or obedience. Rather, their return was a merciful act of their Heavenly Father who loved them in spite of their ongoing failure to live the way He called them to live.

The middle part of Haggai 2 that we read in yesterday indicates their neglect to rebuild the temple had defiled the people. When they resumed the project, God promised to bless them for their obedience. We see that theme in our next passage as well.

> **Read Zechariah 8:1-13.** What message of hope do you see in this passage and who is it for?

> **Read Zechariah 8:14-17.** At the same time, what does Zechariah tell the people to do (and not do)? What does this tell us about them and can you relate in your own life? Why or why not?

Zechariah encouraged them as they continued to rebuild the Temple. He spoke of blessing while calling them to pursue justice and truth, not scheming against others. He told them God would bless them for obedience and that others would see and seek Yahweh, too.

And now, we're going to skip ahead about 100 years to the time when the book of Malachi was written around 430 BC.[iii] Keeping what we just read in Zechariah in mind, see how Malachi's description of the people compares to that.

> **Read Malachi 1:1-5.** What kind of attitude do you see in the people's complaint against God and how does this line up with what we saw in Zechariah?

Remember in session 5 when we read Obadiah and Ezekiel's prophecies of judgment against Edom, Esau's descendants? Without that context, this passage might seem shocking or God's response to the people may seem like it doesn't go with their complaint that God didn't love them.

Read Malachi 1:6-2:17. Again, keeping in mind that this is about a century after the exile ended, what do you notice in Malachi's messages to the people? What impact did the exile have on them?

As I read these chapters, I get the sense that the people of Malachi's day did not have a right view of God. Perhaps they didn't believe He's all-powerful because if He were, why had an enemy conquered them? Perhaps they'd lost any sense of thankfulness the remnant that returned may have had. Overall, it seems like they were simply going through religious motions, but with hearts that weren't fundamentally changed by the exile any more than the people of Zechariah's day (who had experienced the exile and return firsthand).

As I think about how this applies to my own life, it makes me pause. I have significant personal milestones in my walk with the LORD, times when I clearly saw His hand at work in my life. However, do I live my daily life in a way that reflects that understanding of who He is and a thankfulness for the way He's been my provider? Or, like the people of Malachi's day, do I go through the motions without letting God's love and His design for my life really impact my day-to-day choices?

> What impact do difficult times usually have on you? Where may you be off track or have strayed from what God wants you to do? Where may you need to repent or make a change?

PRAYER FOCUS

As you think about those same questions and how they apply to you, spend time reflecting and praying about whether there are any changes you may need to make. Are there areas where you may know the right thing, but aren't living it out? Or like the people's first complaint in Malachi 1:2-5 about whether God really loved them, do you really believe God is who He says He is, that He loves you and is your faithful provider? Ask Him to show you anything you may need to recognize in your own heart or where you may need to make changes.

The Blessing

"Do not be afraid, for I have ransomed you.
    I have called you by name; you are mine.
When you go through deep waters,
    I will be with you.
When you go through rivers of difficulty,
    you will not drown.
When you walk through the fire of oppression,
    you will not be burned up;
    the flames will not consume you.
For I am the LORD, your God,
    the Holy One of Israel, your Savior."
    – Isaiah 43:1b-3a

In 2020 as the pandemic unfolded, a beautiful thing started spreading as church buildings were closed. A song called *The Blessing* became an anthem recorded in individual homes and studios but put together into a video montage. Each video had countless voices all singing the same song of blessing over God's people. (As I write this, they're still available if you search for "The Blessing" on YouTube.) I both sang and cried as I watched video after video of these different groups of believers, separate but united.

The words reminded me that with each new generation, God raises up more of His children to know and follow Him around the world. And each successive generation still receives God's promise of hope. This tradition of passing down words of hope to those that come after us is not new, as the messages in Isaiah 40-66 show.

And so, as we near the end of our time together, we're going to do something a little different today. You'll still see reminders of the warning and judgment part of the prophetic message in what we read, but what you'll see most clearly are words of hope that have been a huge encouragement to me over the years. Though written long ago, they still speak to the situations we face today and show the character of our holy God.

I have a few reflection questions at the end but want you to focus on soaking in the meaning of the words as you read. And as you go, pause if you feel God tugging at your heart as you read a particular passage. It's okay if you don't finish all of these in one sitting or even all in one day. As I've read and reread Isaiah over the years, I'll have days when I can't get past even a couple verses because of how powerfully they speak to me at that time. I've listed a few of these 26 chapters below, but you won't be disappointed if you read all of them!

> Read any or all of the following passages, and jot down anything that stands out to you as you read.

- o **Isaiah 43:1-44:5**

- o **Isaiah 49**

- o **Isaiah 54-55**

- o **Isaiah 61-62**

What theme(s) stood out to you the most?

How do the promises in these passages apply to your life today?

PRAYER FOCUS

Reflecting on what you read, spend time in prayer, thanking God for the promises in these passages. At the same time, in which area(s) do you need hope today? Are you walking through anything that causes you to struggle to believe God has good in store for you? Ask Him to help you see the truth of these passages in your own life.

DAY 5

IN ADVANCE

"For a child is born to us,
a son is given to us.
The government will rest on his shoulders.
And he will be called:
Wonderful Counselor, Mighty God,
Everlasting Father, Prince of Peace.
His government and its peace
will never end.
He will rule with fairness and justice from the throne of his ancestor David
for all eternity.
The passionate commitment of the LORD of Heaven's Armies
will make this happen!"
– Isaiah 9:6-7

Today is our last day together! I'm so thankful you joined me on this journey and hope it spoke to you as you read. I also hope it sparked your interest in going back and reading more in the prophets. They truly are some of my favorite books, filled with so much richness and reminders of God's truth.

Just like yesterday, we're going to spend today looking at the third part of the prophetic message, hope. But this time, we're going to focus on passages where that future hope ultimately points us to the Messiah, Jesus. As you read, look for connections to the New Testament and ways Jesus fulfilled these prophecies. We'll start with the closing verses of the Old Testament in Malachi 4 and an angel visit in Luke 1.

Read Malachi 4. What stands out to you in this passage?

There was a nearly 400-year silence between the end of Malachi and the beginning of Luke when an angel surprised Zechariah while he served in the temple.[iv]

Read Luke 1:5-17. Looking specifically at verse 17, what connection do you see between Malachi 4:5-6 and Luke 1?

The angel told Zechariah he would have a son who would do exactly what Malachi prophesied centuries before. This is just the start of where we see that God made promises through the prophets hundreds of years in advance that would *all* later be fulfilled by Jesus.

Just as in the example we just read where Luke 1 quotes from Malachi 4 and shows the fulfillment of that prophecy, more of these connections can be found throughout the prophetic books we've been studying.

Choose a few of the following passages and jot down what you notice as you read. If your Bible has a concordance or using an online tool like the Bible Hub, you can cross-reference these to places where they're fulfilled in the New Testament.

○ **Isaiah 7:10-16**

○ **Isaiah 9:1-7**

○ **Isaiah 11**

○ **Isaiah 52:13-53:12**

○ **Jeremiah 23:5-8**

○ **Jeremiah 33:14-26**

○ **Zechariah 12:10-13:1**

○ **Isaiah 42:1-4**

○ **Isaiah 59:15-21**

o   **Ezekiel 34**

What connections stood out to you between these passages?

What stood out to you the most as you read?

Overall, the greatest words of hope to everyone, everywhere, are all about Jesus. These prophecies in the Old Testament didn't call Him by name, but just as the angel told Zechariah he would have a son who would fulfill Malachi 4:5-6, Jesus fulfilled what was promised about the coming savior.

And sadly, just as was foretold, He suffered and took our punishment—by *His* stripes we are healed.[v] Yes, we have all failed to live by God's standards and all are guilty of judgment. But God still promises hope to us today. Because Jesus paid the price for us, we can be reconciled to God and we have His Spirit poured out on us. What an amazing, incredible gift!

Looking back over this study overall, what impacted you the most?

What hope have you seen for yourself today through reading these prophetic books from so long ago?

As we wrap up our study, I hope you've seen more of who God is and the hope we have in Him. I also hope you've seen how these prophetic books connect to other parts of the Bible and how they illustrate God's heart for His people. We didn't read every chapter, but if you go back and read each book from start to finish, you'll see even more examples of the prophetic message, more links to other parts of the Old Testament, and more prophecies fulfilled in the New Testament. Above all, I hope doing this study has encouraged you to keep reading and studying your Bible and listening to what the Holy Spirit shows you. May we each have ears to hear![vi]

PRAYER FOCUS

Spend time in prayer as you feel led. May God's grace be on you as you continue your journey with the LORD!

Session 6 Group Guide

Before getting together, have everyone complete Session 6.

1.   Open in prayer.

2.   Questions for the group:

   •   What stands out to you about the people who returned to Jerusalem after the Babylonian exile?

   •   Why do you think Haggai and Zachariah got different results than many of the earlier prophets?

   •   Where do you find yourself prone to complaining against God like the people in Malachi's day, questioning God's love or other aspects of His character?

   •   Out of the passages you read in Isaiah 40-66, what stood out to you the most? Why?

   •   How important is it to you to see how Jesus fulfilled prophecies spoken by multiple prophets hundreds of years before His birth? What sticks out to you the most?

   •   Looking back over this study overall, what's your biggest takeaway?

   •   How likely are you to go back and read/study more in the prophetic books? Why?

   •   In what ways does the 3-part prophetic message apply to your life today?

   •   What promises of hope stood out to you the most over the study and why?

Prophets, Kings and Empires: Approximate Timeline

Year	Empire Dominance	Prophets					Kings of Judah	Kings of Israel
783 BC						Jonah	Amaziah	Jeroboam II
750 BC		Isaiah	Hosea	Amos			Uzziah	
746 BC				Micah				Zechariah (6 months)
745 BC	Assyrian Dominance 745–612 BC						Jotham	Shallum (1 month)
742 BC								Menahem
								Pekahiah
							Ahaz	Pekah
								Hoshea
722 BC							Hezekiah	
715 BC								**No more kings of Israel after Samaria's fall to Assyria in 722 BC
687 BC						Joel (?)		
642 BC						Nahum	Manasseh	
640 BC							Amon	
612 BC		Jeremiah				Zephaniah	Josiah	
609 BC	Babylonian Dominance 612–539 BC		Habakkuk (?)				Jehoahaz (3 months)	
598 BC					Daniel		Jehoiakim	
						Joel (?)	Jehoiachin (3 months)	
586 BC			Ezekiel				Zedekiah	
						Obadiah	**No more kings of Judah after the fall of Jerusalem to Babylon in 586 BC.	
539 BC								
520 BC	Persian Dominance 539–336 BC	Haggai	Zechariah			Joel (?)		
~430 B		Malachi						

150   Session 6: The Remnant Returns

Endnotes

Session 1

[i] "Literary Styles in the Bible," The Bible Project, accessed June 27, 2020, https://bibleproject.com/explore/video/literary-styles-bible/.

[ii] "Literary Styles."

[iii] "Prophet, noun," Merriam-Webster, accessed February 18, 2022, https://www.merriam-webster.com/dictionary/prophet.

[iv] Hays, *The Message of the Prophets*, p. 63. Hays refers back to the three-part message throughout his book as he discusses each of the prophets, but he introduces it on page 63.

[v] J. Daniel Hays, *The Message of the Prophets: A Survey of the Prophetic and Apocalyptic Books of the Old Testament*, ed. Tremper Longman, III. (Michigan: Zondervan Academic, 2010), p. 260 and James D. Nogalski, *Introduction to the Hebrew Prophets*. (Nashville: Abingdon Press, 2018), p. 200.

[vi] "Introduction to the Hebrew Bible".

[vii] "Books of the Tanakh" in *The Complete Jewish Study Bible*, ed. Rabbi Barry Rubin (Massachusetts: Hendrickson Publishers Marketing, LLC, 2016), p. x.

[viii] "Introduction to the Hebrew Bible," The Bible Project, March 2020, https://bibleproject.com/course/hebrew-bible-full-class/.

[ix] "Introduction to the Hebrew Bible".

[x] James D. Nogalski, *Introduction to the Hebrew Prophets*. (Nashville: Abingdon Press, 2018), p. xv.

[xi] "Introduction to the Complete Jewish Bible" in *The Complete Jewish Study Bible*, ed. Rabbi Barry Rubin (Massachusetts: Hendrickson Publishers Marketing, LLC, 2016), viii & xxxvii.

[xii] Hays, *The Message of the Prophets*, p. xv-xx.

[xiii] "Introduction to the Hebrew Bible", Lesson 15.

[xiv] "Introduction to the Hebrew Bible", Lesson 15.

[xv] "Poetry," Wikipedia, accessed June 30, 2021, https://en.m.wikipedia.org/wiki/Poetry.

[xvi] Hays, *The Message of the Prophets*, p. 48

[xvii] Hays, *The Message of the Prophets*, p. 48

[xviii] Hays, *The Message of the Prophets*, p. 49

[xix] *The Complete Jewish Study Bible*, xli.

[xx] While the examples are different, the format mirrors a table found in *The Complete Jewish Study Bible*, p. xlii.

[xxi] Hays, *The Message of the Prophets*, p. 51.

[xxii] Poetry type definitions came from Hays, *The Message of the Prophets*, p. 53-56.

[xxiii] "Introduction to the Hebrew Bible".

[xxiv] Hays, *The Message of the Prophets*, p. 56-57.

[xxv] "Moresheth-Gath," *Wikipedia*, accessed October 15, 2022, https://en.wikipedia.org/wiki/Moresheth-Gath

[xxvi] Hays, *The Message of the Prophets*, p. 34.

[xxvii] Hays, *The Message of the Prophets*, p. 266.
[xxviii] See 2 Chronicles 36:2 and 36:9.

Session 2

[i] See Matthew 2:13-20.
[ii] See Amos 1:1 and Amos 7:14.
[iii] Hays, *The Message of the Prophets*, p. 286.
[iv] Hays, *The Message of the Prophets*, p. 287.
[v] Hays, *The Message of the Prophets*, p. 38.
[vi] See Job 38:4-7; Psalm 65:6 & 135:7; Isaiah 40:12 & 47:4, Jeremiah 10:13, 16 & 13:16; Daniel 2:28, 30; Joel 2:2; Amos 5:8, 27 & 9:6; and Micah 1:3.
[vii] Hays, *The Message of the Prophets*, p. 310.
[viii] See Jeremiah 26.
[ix] Hays, *The Message of the Prophets*, p. 310.
[x] See 1 Kings 16:21-33
[xi] "Omri, King of Israel," *Encyclopedia Britannica*, accessed September 25, 2021, https://www.britannica.com/biography/Omri.
[xii] See Numbers 22-24 for the full story.
[xiii] Hays, *The Message of the Prophets*, p. 300.
[xiv] Hays, *The Message of the Prophets*, p. 300.
[xv] Erika Belibtreu, "Grisly Assyrian Record of Torture and Death," *Biblical Archaeology Society*, accessed October 17, 2021, https://faculty.uml.edu/ethan_spanier/Teaching/documents/CP6.0AssyrianTorture.pdf

Session 3

[i] See 2 Kings 14:24-18 and 15:8-31.
[ii] Scripture taken from the NEW AMERICAN STANDARD BIBLE®, Copyright © 1960, 1962, 1963, 1968, 1971, 1973, 1975, 1977, 1995 By The Lockman Foundation. Used by permission.
[iii] "NASB: Lexicon – Isaiah 26:3," *Bible Hub*, accessed October 3, 2021, https://biblehub.com/lexicon/isaiah/26-3.htm.
[iv] "Interlinear Bible – Isaiah 10," *Bible Hub*, accessed October 17, 2021, https://biblehub.com/interlinear/isaiah/10.htm.
[v] For more details, see Isaiah 36-37, 2 Kings 18-19, and 2 Chronicles 32.
[vi] J Daniel Hays, & Tremper Longman, III. (2010). *The message of the prophets: a survey of the prophetic and apocalyptic books of the Old Testament.* Zondervan Academic.
[vii] Hays, *The Message of the Prophets*, p.40. and Nogalski, *Hebrew Prophets*, p. 135-136.
[viii] Ellicott's Commentary for English Readers – Bible Hub
[ix] Nogalski, *Introduction to the Hebrew Prophets*, p. 129-130.
[x] Hays, *The Message of the Prophets*, p. 336.
[xi] Hays, *The Message of the Prophets*, p.339. and Nogalski, *Hebrew Prophets*, p.135.

xii "Strong's Concordance – 8193. Saphah" *Bible* Hub, accessed October 27, 2021, https://biblehub.com/hebrew/8193.htm.

xiii Hays, *The Message of the Prophets*, p.339.

xiv Hays, *The Message of the Prophets*, p.339.

xv "Ellicott's Commentary for English Readers," *Bible Hub*, accessed January 28, 2022, https://biblehub.com/commentaries/2_kings/21-16.htm.

xvi "Commentary on 2 Kings 21:16," *Bible Hub*, accessed January 28, 2022, https://biblehub.com/commentaries/2_kings/21-16.htm.

Session 4

i Hays, *The Message of the Prophets*, p. 322.

ii Hays, *The Message of the Prophets*, p. 41.

iii

iv

v Dr. Caroline Leaf, "Introduction" in *Switch on Your Brain*, p. 22-28. & Dr. Bessel van der Kolk, "Applied Neuroscience" in *The Body Keeps the Score*, p. 316.

vi Hays, *The Message of the Prophets*, p. 276.

Session 5

i Hays, *The Message of the Prophets*, p. 40.

ii Hays, *The Message of the Prophets*, p. 40.

iii Hays, *The Message of the Prophets*, p. 40-41.

iv See 2 Kings 24:8-17.

v Hays, *The Message of the Prophets*, p. 41.

vi See also Ezekiel 35.

vii Leaf, "How and Why the 21-Day Brain Detox Plain Works" in *Switch on Your Brain*, p. 150.

viii *Holy Bible,* New Living Translation. (Illinois: Tyndale House Publishers, Inc., 2012), p. 255.

ix *Holy Bible*, NLT, p. 255.

Session 6

i Hays, *The Message of the Prophets*, p. 41.

ii Hays, *The Message of the Prophets*, p. 356.

iii Hays, *The Message of the Prophets*, p. 360.

iv According to Hays, *The Message of the Prophets*, p. 360, Malachi was written around 430 BC.

v Isaiah 53:5

vi See Matthew 11:15, Ezekiel 3:7, and Revelation 2:7.

Timeline

i In 750 BC Jotham became co-regent with Uzziah according to Hays, *The Message of the Prophets*, p. 266. See also 2 Kings 15:3-5 and 2 Chronicles 26:16-23.

Made in the USA
Las Vegas, NV
13 February 2023

67435849R00085